IFEOMA NDIOLO

YOU

TOO

CAN

Overcome life's challenges

Published by
AMV Publishing Services
259 Nassau Street Ste 2 #661
Princeton NJ 08542-4609
Tel: + 1 609-627-9168 - Fax: + 1 609-716-7224
emails: publisher@amvpublishingservices.com &
customerservice@amvpublishingservices.com
worldwide web: https://amvpublishingservices.com

You Too Can Overcome Life's Struggles

Book & Cover Design: AMV Origination & Design Division

Library of Congress Control Number: 2024933620

ISBN: 978-978-604-647-1.

For Adaora …. You are the pride of my life

CONTENTS

ACKNOWLEDGEMENT

A special thank you to my Lord Jesus Christ for the miracles in my life and for helping me overcome the challenges I have faced. I am grateful to my parents, Mrs. Mary Magdalene Chibuaku Ndiolo and Chief Godwin Ukeje Ndiolo for being my first teachers and for the virtues they taught me that helped me to deal with life's issues. They were my first teachers. They continued to influence my life with wisdom until they were called from the earth. I appreciate my daughter, Adaora for making the best of God's blessings upon our lives. I will forever be thankful to all the angels that God sent my way to help me walk through my life's journey. My sister Chizo, my friend Uche and her sister Nkechi. My friends Pearl, Tonia, Rebecca, Tina, Dr George Okwerekwu and his wife Dr Irene Okwerekwu. You all, in different ways made my dreams come true. I deeply appreciate my friend, Mrs. Folasade Adefisayo for making this publication possible. I am thankful for all the work done by my publisher, Damola Ifaturoti, and his team at AMV Publishing Services. Your amazing dedication to success saw this through.

PRELUDE

This book is for you if you are facing challenges in your life and wish to rise above the limitations. You should dare to be different. What you need is faith. Walk with conviction, trusting God and with a positive mindset. You will succeed.

I must admit that I have lived quite an interesting life, a life full of adventure. I was born and nurtured in a family environment that made me imbibe such versatility which prepared me to be able to blend with citizens of diverse cultures. I was also fortunate enough to have been so multi-talented that I was able to take up different kinds of employment. From working as a News Reporter for a TV station, I became a marketer for a bank. From banking, I moved over to the insurance industry where I trained and mentored younger marketers for decades. That was before I discovered advertising and the health industry. My life has never really been static. Rather, it has been embellished with various incidents, pleasant and unpleasant, from which I learned how to better prepare myself for the purpose for which I was created, which is to help others that are encountering and battling through challenges in their lives.

My late father, Chief Godwin Ukeje Ndiolo, was a civil servant who used to travel from one location to another. He usually took us and our mother along with him. That was how I discovered that the world was much bigger than I imagined. From reading many books and watching movies at a young age, I began to dream of venturing out of my immediate environment. I decided that I needed to explore the rest of the unknown world. By sending me to four primary schools and two secondary schools in different locations, my father assisted in broadening my dreams. I also attended two universities, one for my first degree and the second for a master's degree.

After graduation, I worked in different sections of the economy; media, banking, advertising, and insurance. In those schools and offices, I came across various kinds of people with whom I interacted on daily basis. I learned so much while going through life that I stored up sufficient knowledge to influence other people. I also realized that I enjoyed the adventure that came with traveling because it gave me the opportunity to discover new cultures, languages, and food in the countries I visited.

As I matured and consciously continued to write, I formed the habit of packing a jotter in my bag, before embarking on any journey. Whenever the urge to put pen to paper became irresistible, I scribbled down my thoughts. Fortunately, I had long realized that the worst thing that could happen to a writer was not being able to capture a striking thought the moment it ran through one's mind. Most often than not, one would never be able to recall that idea in the way and manner it first came.

Recently, I was distressed for days while trying to recall the first line of a poem that I was so compelled to write about a pathetic incident that affected some citizens of my country, Nigeria. Some Nigerians living in South Africa were being murdered. Unfortunately, I did not take notes when the thought of writing the poem first came to me. It took me over two days to recall the exact words I wanted to use. Jotting down ideas and information that I want to remember, has always been of great advantage to me.

It was while waiting for my flight at the Kotoka international airport, Accra, in the year 2010, on one of my numerous trips from the capital city of Ghana that I began to write this book. On this journey to Lagos, my flight was delayed for three inexplicable hours. All through this period, no airline official bothered to explain the reason for the delay to the passengers. An hour after we were to have departed, I heard some of the passengers who scheduled appointments in Lagos murmuring and lamenting loudly about their situation. While many of them were trying to occupy themselves with their laptops, novels and magazines, others shut their eyes and slept, clutching on to their handbags and luggage.

A tall, well-built man walked over to one of the airline officials and demanded an explanation; his response was a lame "the plane had not arrived from Lagos." The man was visibly angry, but managed to control himself. He took a deep breath and returned to his seat. As a frequent traveler, I had experienced delayed flights too often that I decided not to dwell on the situation, but to make the best use of the waiting time. I knew that the best solution for such a time waster was to engage in something productive. I dug out my jotter and began to write. That was how I avoided feeling frustrated until the aircraft was available and ready for boarding. If you can find ways to prevent events happening around you from adversely affecting your temperament, then you have found the key to avoiding frustration.

In this book, I have compiled certain ideologies that guided me through the challenges I had to face as my life evolved. I have revealed how I was able to overcome them, while realizing that when properly handled, life's challenges become less burdensome and therefore easier to overcome.

Here you will find the principles I believed in and practiced, and an exposition of some of my true-life experiences, you will also discover how the principles helped me and some people close to me to survive difficult situations.

It is my sincere hope that you will enjoy going through these experiences with me and learn one or two things while we are on this trip. I also expect that you will be convinced enough to imbibe a fearless and never give up attitude that will help you develop a strong faith in God when you read **YOU TOO CAN.**

THE POWER IS WITHIN YOU

The power to determine the course of your life is entirely within you. God has given you everything you need to be successful; but it is up to you to make the decision to succeed or not. Within every human being is the ability to reason, and the human brain is so well equipped for this purpose. Man was given eyes for seeing and ears for hearing. Animals function differently. While some are unable to see colors, others are color blind. No matter how smart they seem to be, they cannot hear or speak the language of man. A parrot, which is considered a very intelligent bird, can only mimic man. Every human being has talents. There is absolutely no man that is born without a talent. The responsibility lies on every one of us to make a deliberate effort to discover our talents and work towards developing them. The realization that man was created for a purpose should make everyone strive to sharpen and utilize his talent in a way that will make him live a productive life.

You Too Can Overcome Life's Challenges

In a world full of challenges, insufficiency, and constant depletion of resources, it is easier and much more convenient to sit back and churn out excuses, while waiting for things to happen. Unfortunately, things do not just happen. You and I must make them happen. It is true that everyone wants to win the lottery and have an opportunity of living a life of luxury without slaving for it. We are also aware that some people waited for miracles throughout their lifetime and died without moving from point A to B.

Miracles do happen but they can only happen when you have faith. However, most people must work extra hard before being able to afford bare necessities. Making a success of your life does not always have to be that difficult. Do not sit around waiting for miracles, do something about your situation. Start by defining your purpose, designing your plan, making some choices, and formulating your strategies. All you need to do is to stay focused and take the necessary steps required towards achieving a resounding success.

DEFINE YOUR PURPOSE

DESIGN YOUR PLAN

MAKE YOUR CHOICES

FORMULATE STRATEGIES

STAY FOCUSED

EXECUTE YOUR PLAN

ACHIEVE SUCCESS

I spent a good number of years procrastinating and believing that situations would always take care of themselves. I thought that if I worked hard enough, there was no reason why I should not be successful. As the years went by, I realized that if I really wanted to succeed, it was up to me to begin to make the right choices. These were choices relating to how I wanted my life to be, and what shape as well as pattern the rest of my life would take. I knew then that I had to take certain steps towards achieving my personal goals and started doing so. These were some of the principles that helped me to overcome the challenges I faced and I highly recommend them to you.

CHAPTER 1

CHOOSE TO BE HAPPY

> "ALL SEASONS ARE BEAUTIFUL FOR THE PERSON WHO CARRIES HAPPINESS WITHIN" – HORACE FRIESS

I used to frown more often than I smiled. Frowning was one of the tactics I adopted as a young girl for warding off male admirers, who by my understanding, were threatening to constitute a diversion that could prevent me from concentrating on my studies. I realized that when a girl frowns, fewer boys have the courage to approach her. I considered the time my female friends spent chatting with male admirers as a time waster. It worked at the time, because reducing "chit – chat" time meant more time for reading. I loved to read so much that I was willing to sacrifice my meals.

As I grew older, this once useful strategy almost turned me into a recluse. I had developed a very serious nature that I needed to deliberately lose. I had to learn how to open my heart and mind to accommodate other people, who were willing to share their lives with me. I also began to learn how to be more friendly, flexible, and adaptable to situations. I learned how to laugh again. Through laughing, I began to find pleasure in situations and eventually became a much happier person.

Laughter, they say is the best medicine. It is also said that the best things in life are free. That must explain why laughter is free. Laughter is a priceless, easy to obtain free medicine, which so many people fail to take advantage of throughout their earthly sojourn. I have often wondered why some people prefer to frown instead of laugh, when it is much easier to laugh. I once considered if they had more reasons to frown than to laugh or if their lives were worse off. I eventually concluded that it is neither of the two. There are more reasons in life to laugh than to frown. Bad things do not happen to anyone on daily basis.

There are times when people go through weeks or months without having any negative experience. When you look around you, and your loved ones are healthy, why not laugh and glorify God. You should indeed thank God for his blessings and compassion towards you for every day you exist on earth. When you can appreciate God's love and endless compassion, you will find reasons to laugh all the time. Besides, it does not cost anyone a dime to laugh. Laughter is free.

If that is not sufficient reason for you, then here is another reason why you should learn to laugh. Acknowledge whom you truly are – God's own child, formed in his very image, filled with his spirit, and bestowed with heavenly powers. This will make you not to ever have a reason to worry. Appreciating what God has blessed you with and all that you have become, will make you continue to laugh even when there seems to be no reason for you to do so. There is every reason to laugh.

Scientists have been able to prove that it requires less muscles to laugh than to frown. Laughing, is a matter of choice. That may explain why two people who are in a similar situation react in different ways. While one person finds a reason to burst out laughing, the other person maintains a straight face. In such a situation, an observer may decide that the person that did not laugh either missed the humor in the situation, or despises laughter. It is possible that he could not appreciate the beauty of that moment because he was too busy brooding over his problems. That may be why even in an auditorium filled with many people, watching a performing comedian; while some are practically jumping off their seats in excitement, you may still find others who are not laughing.

I have long realized that there is so much humor around us. All you need to do is pay attention to your surroundings and you will be cracking up with laughter. You can start from listening to your children, to reading the inscription at the back of commercial buses and noting the errors on them. You can read sign posts and advertorials on bill boards. You can check out graffiti on the walls and those legitimate and illegitimate adverts on people's walls. There are so many interesting things to notice and to laugh about.

People, who have decided to be happy, find reasons to laugh. They live longer because they enjoy the simplest things that nature freely provides. They also look younger than those who are always serious and continue to frown for no reason. A smile goes a long way in lifting not just our moods but also that of the people around us. Even if you do not feel like laughing or smiling, do it for the sake of others. There are too many people overburdened by life issues. You can lighten their burden by having a pleasant disposition. Determine today to brighten up every room you walk into and you will begin to realize the advantage of such a positive attitude.

A smile not only opens doors for you, it can win contracts. Besides, you can ease other people's sorrows by smiling and by so doing make them realize that the world is not as terrible as it may sometimes seem. I urge you to learn from me. I am never bored. I make sure I entertain myself wherever I may be and despite whatever challenge I may be facing. I make sure I utilize my time well by doing something productive.

Being happy is a choice that one makes and then sets out to achieve. I am certain that the choices people make and the way they react to events around them, determine what their lives turn out to be. Their choices also dictate if they live a fulfilled life or not. People, who have chosen to be happy, somehow rise above all sorts of misery, deprivation, and poverty. They continue to laugh, celebrate events, and generate multiple ways of relaxation; thereby easing off tension, remaining healthy and living longer than others. While it is a fact that people's opinions, actions, and reactions are mostly because of their perception of events that occur around them, it is also true that perception differs from one person to another.

The way you perceive a particular situation can be very different from the way someone else perceives it. It is therefore important for you to be very careful and apply restraint when necessary, so as not to end up over - reacting to events that happen either to you or to other people around you. You have a clear choice. You can either choose to react, over - react, or do absolutely nothing about a situation. It is important to note that how you choose to respond determines what happens next in the chain of events.

A woman who has just been insulted by her neighbor decides to empty a kettle of hot water on her head. While she has every reason to be offended by her neighbor's behavior, she has over – reacted by physically assaulting her neighbor and should be ready to face the consequences of her action. The victim may involve the police who will arrest her. She may be found guilty and will suffer the stipulated penalty for such an offence. If she is lucky, the police may eventually release her for lack of evidence. Whichever way the judgment goes, she can never really go unpunished. Due to her reaction, she has destroyed a relationship for life. The same woman could have calmed down and allowed her anger to dissipate, thereby creating an opportunity for peacemakers to intervene. She would probably have received an apology from her neighbor and given peace a chance to reign in their relationship.

The same applies to a husband who catches another man sleeping with his wife. He may decide to kill the man, beat up his wife, and, or divorce her. Whichever decision he takes has consequences attached to it and the man's life would probably never remain the same. His reaction will determine how badly he suffers. The truth is that his reaction to the incident can hurt him much more than his wife's unfaithfulness ever did. It is bad enough that his wife broke his heart by committing adultery. The question however is, should he walk away, or should he incur a prison term or even a death penalty by committing murder or limit his suffering to the pains of a broken heart. The choice is his and unfortunately, he has only a few seconds within which to make that fundamental decision.

No matter how angry you are, you must learn how to control your emotions. It is true that you are human and are prone to react to situations, but you can manage your emotions and respond with your head instead of your heart. Let us further examine this unfortunate man's peculiar situation:

FACT: His wife has been cheating on him

FACT: She betrayed him

FACT: He cannot trust her anymore

FACT: He must decide on whether to continue to live with her or not

FACT: His life must go on

Even if he kills the male adulterer, or both, it will not obliterate the incident. He has other options. He can take time out to think about the situation and come up with a logical solution. He can decide to forgive her and give her another chance, so that they can continue their lives as a couple and raise their children together. Over time, if she is truly repentant, they will learn to forget the past and pick up the pieces of their lives. It all depends on the choice he makes after the incident occurred.

Although many men will opt for divorce so that the society will not see them as foolish, they will also not want to become a laughing stock to their neighbors. It however, remains entirely up to the man to make a choice. Providence has shown that lots of men and women, who forgive their spouses for infidelity, end up not regretting their decision. The truly repentant ones stay faithful and grateful for the rest of their lives while using every precious moment to make up for that moment of indiscretion.

With all the problems we must grapple with in this world, one can only imagine what life would be like if we choose to create more misery around us. If everyone was sad, miserable, and unhappy, life would certainly be very boring. Many men are living very unhappy lives. They have chosen to be miserable and may never even realize it until it is too late. For such people, by the time they eventually come to terms with the damage they have perpetrated upon themselves, they would be struck with various types of diseases. Only then will they realize that if they had made more sensible choices, their lives would have turned out better. By then, it will be too late to reverse the situation.

I used to be uptight, taking life and everything relating to it too serious. I got easily angry. I reacted to the slightest provocation. I was too emotional. If you made me a promise and failed to keep it, it seemed like you pierced my heart with a knife. I was also an exceptionally clean person. My house had to be spic and span with no speck of dust or cobwebs. If I saw a cobweb, I would jump up immediately and reach for the cobweb broom. From clearing the cobwebs, I would discover the dust on the shelves and the duster would follow immediately.

I remember how a friend of mine visited one day and went to use my bathroom. When she was done, she asked me a very surprising question:

'Do you take your bath in there?'

She did not understand how a bathroom used every day could have been that clean. She insisted on being lectured on how to take proper care of bathrooms. That was several years ago.

My dressing table was so well arranged that if you came to my room and saw a deodorant in any position, you were sure to return three weeks later, and find it at that same spot. Another friend requested explanation of how I picked up my body cream each day and returned it to the same spot, after use. My friends and relatives staying with me or visiting had to learn how to ensure that my house remained neat and tidy. Were they truly happy with me for my uppity attitude, there was no way I could tell, and sincerely, I was never bothered about it. I was so concerned about ensuring that my environment was super clean that I was prepared to make everyone uncomfortable until I achieved my aim.

With time, I learned how to relax and take things slightly easier. Although I keep my house and surroundings clean, I learned how to ignore certain things around me until I had the energy to tackle them. I must admit that it was not easy for me because I still loathe any form of dirt or disorder, but it was necessary. I began to make the required changes when a doctor erroneously informed me, that I had developed a heart problem. My boyfriend at the time installed a bell by my bedside, to ensure that I did not have to yell when I needed anything. He taught me how to take things easy and cautioned me gently when I attempted to yell like I used to.

He was so nice about it that I became convinced that it was ultimately in my best interest to stop worrying too much. He was also able to persuade me that he meant well by showing an unusual interest in my health. Not only did he take me to his family doctor; he also paid my medical bills. This genuine show of affection softened my doggedness and I began to relax better with my friends and family. I became so transformed that much as I would deliberately not entertain a dirty environment, I refused to allow any disorderliness interrupt my rest.

Gradually, I began to learn how not to get angry over events happening around me and to stay calm even when the whole world seemed to be collapsing. I learned to quietly counsel myself and react in ways that did not jeopardize my health. As time went on, I got so used to the new me and found out that I could utilize most of the energy I expended on yelling at people on more productive ventures. By insisting on not getting upset over everything that went wrong around me and being able to choose when to react or not, I was able to better tolerate other people's whims and caprices. In a short while, it became obvious that taking that decision made me a better woman.

It was an event that occurred during the production of my Television Drama Series, Pawns, that made me further realize how much I had altered my life. We had just returned from a location in Lagos, where we worked overnight. We came back in a convoy, as was always the case (for security purposes). The location bus drove next to my car, to drop off some members of the crew who opted to sleep over in my house.

It was in the wee hours of the morning and it was not safe for them to return to their various homes. Every member of the cast and crew was exhausted, with tempers flying. As if we had not had enough drama, the assistant cameraman decided to confiscate my master tapes. His reason was that my production manager (PM) did not pay him the full amount of money negotiated for the job. Before I knew what was happening, a scuffle had ensued between him and my Production Manager, who was insisting on retrieving the tapes from him.

I asked my PM to back off and let the cameraman go with the tapes. Perplexed and very disappointed, he asked if I meant that he should allow the cameraman walk away with my master tapes. My response was an emphatic yes. I told him to get into the house and locked my gate. He was still fuming and looking confused as the location bus drove away with the cameraman feeling very good with himself.

Unknown to them all, I was sure that I had something over the cameraman. I knew he would turn up the following day to collect his outstanding payment. I was convinced that in his best interests, he would not damage, destroy, or misplace my tapes. Besides, he was very much aware of the value of the tapes and could not even begin to imagine what might happen to him if anything went wrong with them. He was therefore duty bound to take the best possible care of the tapes. A fact I thought through. One, which my PM did not consider, because he was too busy getting unnecessarily furious with him.

The following day, my PM was shocked when the cameraman not only returned the tapes but also tendered an unreserved apology for his behavior, before collecting his outstanding balance.

You Too Can Overcome Life's Challenges

Getting angry with people who deliberately try to infuriate you is not necessary. When you identify a particular person or people who always try to get on your nerves, you owe it to yourself not to let them succeed in making you sad. Happiness is truly a choice. Over time, I have learned that the people we meet as we carry on our day-to-day activities have different roles to play in our lives. While some are available to make us happy, others are there to upset us. While some people praise and encourage us, several others insult and try to bring us down. While we have people that like us, many others despise us. The rest really do not care whether we succeed or not.

While some people are encouraging us to grow, others work towards our downfall and enjoy watching us go through pain. Bearing in mind that it is not our creator's will for us to suffer unnecessarily, we owe it to ourselves to make the choices that will ensure that we do not. Despite the type of people we encounter in our lives and no matter their motive, it is our duty to insist on not allowing them to make us miserable. If you decide to be happy, you will see how different your life will become. You will not only be able to influence the lives of people around you; they will learn so much from your life style.

Happiness is very important for a successful life and can spread from you to others around you. It is only when you achieve an inner wellbeing of happiness, that you can to make people around you happy. You will not only be able to ignore negative character traits and behavioral patterns but will also relate with such individuals courteously and without prejudice. I can confidently tell you this, because I have experienced it. If you can do this, it makes the person that had been mean to you, and who you rewarded with kindness, feel petty and mean. You seem larger than life to him, leaving him in awe of your ability to be good to him when he obviously did not deserve it.

Unknown to him, by treating him with kindness, you have done yourself a lot of good. You have relieved yourself from the burden of carrying an unforgiving baggage that could weigh you down for a very long time.

Life is short. You owe it to yourself to make every effort to be happy at home and at work. At most, you live to be a hundred years or a little more. In those short years on earth, try and make people around you happy. When it comes to happiness, what you sow is what you reap. If you are good, good things will come your way. It may not come from those you have treated well, but your reward will come in your life time. On the other hand, if you are wicked, you will surely face the repercussion as well. Karma is real.

Happiness is a decision which you must make for yourself. Ensure that no one makes you unhappy, even when they try. Sincerely, no one has the right to make you unhappy. You must learn how to protect yourself from the wickedness that exists in the world we live to be able to enjoy the beauty that abounds in it. Your heart is your stronghold and the center of your happiness. You must know how to protect it. Therefore, let certain experiences bounce off your skin. Do not let them touch your heart.

The key to happiness is being able to forgive those who hurt you and looking up to God for solace and comfort. Do not depend on man, but put your trust in God. When your expectation from people is high, you get easily disappointed. I am not advising that you should become an island. You must necessarily relate with people. Remember, someone gave birth to you and nurtured you when you were helpless. There is a reason why you were born into a family, with parents and siblings. Even if you have no siblings, you have relatives.

The closest people to you sometimes irritate and hurt you. Learn to forgive them. Let your family be your training ground on how to handle the rest of the world. I became a happier person when I decided not to ever get angry with my parents, no matter what they did to me. With my siblings, I decided not to let the anger at the way they treated me affect me. I also chose not to count their offences. That was when I was truly able to love them and relate with them even when they repeatedly hurt me. Your family is your blood; you really cannot cut them off. If you try to end relationship with your family, you will not only hurt them but will also hurt yourself. The same principle should apply to your marriage partner, except when your life is in danger.

The truth is that misery begets health issues. Many men and women are living in miserable homes and enduring unhappiness because of their children. My advice to them is to get help. If love has flown out of your home, do something to wake everybody up instead of keeping quiet and enduring the pain. Your whole family suffers for it. Your health deteriorates. Even your children pay for your complacency, one way or the other. It either affects their health or their personality, forever. Children from miserable homes are never happy. Misery never gives birth to anything good. The ability to recognize situations for what they truly are and formulate strategies to overcome them is the real proof of maturity. Start working on your mental state. When you get to a certain stable stage, no one can make you miserable anymore.

Some people go to work every day in misery and spend all day lamenting their situation. They hate their jobs. Such people often end up with health issues. A workplace is not a war zone. You need to be mentally stable to be able to contribute your best. Learn how to deal with every situation as it comes. Sometimes, you need to speak out. Let your colleagues know that you are aware of what is going on. Do not go fighting anyone but calmly make your point. There are times you must tell people to back off. Believe me, they will, when you do so. I had to tell people who were attacking me at my job to back off and surprisingly it worked. My relationship with the concerned parties improved drastically.

Sometimes, people dump their misery on others. I call it work place abuse. Unfortunately, if you keep taking the abuse, be prepared to take more because it will keep coming. There are bullies everywhere, not just in schools. The day you say no to work abuse it will stop. I have watched some people close to me go through abuse in their work places and my advice to them is always the same – say no to work place abuse. Unfortunately, those who continue to endure, find out that it never stops. Speak out; if it costs you your job then you were meant to have left a while back. Do not worry, most often than not you step into a better job. Do not trade your happiness for a job, it is not worth it.

A similar situation of bullying also exists in places where we live. Some landlords abuse their tenants. Neighbors abuse each other. If you have paid for a space, you should be allowed to enjoy it. If the situation is otherwise, you have every right to protest. We are all not meant to be landlords. Do not consider being a tenant as a curse. The person that is a landlord today was previously a tenant. Do not feel that you need to always apologize for being a tenant. Insist on being happy where you live and work because that is where you spend most of your time. Start by making people around you happy and insist on staying happy. You truly can.

> "HAPPINESS EXISTS ON EARTH, AND IT IS WON THROUGH
> PRUDENT EXERCISE OF REASON, KNOWLEDGE OF THE
> HARMONY OF THE UNIVERSE, AND CONSTANT PRACTICE
> OF GENEROSITY"
> — JOSE MARTI

LESSONS:

- It pays to smile
- Laughter is free medicine
- Everyone you meet in life has a role to play
- A happy person is a more tolerant person
- You can manage your emotions
- Treat people well even when they do not treat you well
- Life is short
- Your heart is your stronghold and the center of your happiness
- Protect your heart from being hurt
- When your expectation is high, you get easily disappointed
- Learn to forgive
- Your family is your blood, you really cannot cut them off
- Misery begets health issues
- If your home is miserable, get help
- Misery never gives birth to anything good
- The ability to recognize situations for what they truly are and formulate strategies to counter them is the real proof of maturity
- A workplace is not a war zone
- Say no to workplace abuse
- Do not trade your happiness for a job, no job is worth it
- Do not apologize for being a tenant
- Insist on being happy where you live and work

CHAPTER 2

MAKE CLEAR CHOICES

> **"LIFE IS THE SUM OF ALL YOUR CHOICES"**
> **– ALBERT CAMUS**

Select your friends carefully. Be a friend to all but be very mindful of those you bring close to your heart or home. Select your best friends even more carefully. Start by looking for people with like minds and align yourself with them. Also, make friends with people you can either learn from or who can influence you. If all your friends know what you know, how can any of you get better?

Your circle of friends should be capable of influencing each other. I recommend that you make friends with people from different age grades. That way, there will be much more excitement in your relationships. People from diverse age grades see things differently. Their ideas differ and they are passionate about different things. If you choose your friends carefully, you will discover that there is always something new to learn from each of them. If you study them and understand their strengths and weaknesses, then you will know who best to lean on, when necessary. There are different kinds of people with diverse temperaments. It is important to know who to gossip with, confide in, and party with. When it comes to executing business projects, you should also diligently select those you can successfully partner with.

No other person determines the path your life takes or what happens to you but yourself. Parents, teachers, friends, neighbors, and the environment influence your life and help in propelling you towards your destiny, they do not ultimately determine who you become. While there is no doubt that they play a major part in preparing you for your roles in life, they neither decide what you do with your life nor decide your future. The onus lies on you to determine what you want to do with your life and how successful you want to become.

As you mature, you realize that you are free to choose from a wide variety of options. You are the person that will decide what type of profession to pursue and how you intend to train for it. You select your friends, business partners and acquaintances. Eventually, you decide who you end up sharing your life with. It is your life and your decision. Every decision you make matters.

When you were a child, your parents taught and guided you. They made you aware of what existed around you. As days went by, you began to observe and understand what was going on around you, especially as you watched them talk. Once you started recognizing colors, you got attracted to them. You started hearing different languages being spoken around you and comprehended the much you could as you blossomed. Eventually, you became more aware of the people and animals around you and this increased your interest in your environment. You began to familiarize yourself with the world, and to discover your immediate surroundings. You explored it, learning from the people you interacted with and the events you witnessed.

That was a very important stage in your life, because what largely forms your opinions and the decisions you will later make in life are those events that took place earlier in your life. They remain in your memory. They help in molding you into whom you eventually become. To prevent your early childhood experiences from negatively influencing your adult life, you need to find the inner strength to fight through the challenges as they unfold. You need to believe in yourself and your ability to overcome them, otherwise you will be helpless and allow the hurdles of life to control you.

Let me explain further. When a child begins to read, write, and watch television, he has a vast opportunity to gather new and unimaginable information. What he learns determines his attitude and perspective. In his innocence, he totally believes and accepts what he sees or hears. The moment he starts school, he travels from his parents' home to a new world of discovery. Whether he becomes artistic or otherwise would depend largely on his understanding and passion for what he sees or hears. The books he reads also have a major role to play in molding him. Using myself as an example, the books I read before adulthood contributed tremendously in turning me into who I later became.

As soon as I began to read and write, a whole new world opened to me. While physically still in my parents' house in Enugu, the capital city of Enugu state – Nigeria, I found myself mentally travelling to so many countries around the world. I discovered new people, cultures, languages, food, and fashion. I even began to design my clothes and sketch my hairstyles. Fortunately, my father's house was well positioned to act as an observatory. It was a corner piece that gave me an opportunity to spend many hours in the day, sitting by the window in our living room to watch commuters passing by. From my vantage position, I could see the road in front and by the side of our home. I saw buses and taxis dropping off passengers and watched private cars driving by. There was always something interesting to observe. Combined with a book in my hand, my life became amazingly very interesting.

I loved reading so much that I almost read every book that I could lay my hands on. As soon as my father noticed my interest in his newspapers and books, he began buying story books for me. The books came in different shapes and colors and became my most precious possession. I cherished every one of them and read them all. He also bought poetry books for me. I developed a keen interest in understanding the meaning of the poems I read. That was when I started memorizing and narrating poems to my siblings. I also entertained my friends with some of the stories in the books. I absolutely enjoyed reading. If you wanted to give me a gift and you chose a book, you were sure to find me dancing with joy. You would realize that you made the best choice.

I can also remember sitting on the floor in my father's living room, surrounded by Daily Newspapers which I devoured, one after the other. I had books that were large volumes; books that some children may not even be willing to read. As a teenager, I was introduced to the Mills and Boon, James Hadley Chase, and Agatha Christie detective series by my school friends. I read every one of them. I followed the stories and eagerly spent my pocket money on those novels. At some point, they became a distraction.

I was able to finish reading one novel in a day. I remember the excitement that gushed through me, while I read through the romance stories of Mills and Boon. You can only imagine the adrenaline that gushed through me as Agatha Christie spurned her tales of murder and James Hadley Chase masterfully told his thriller stories. To me, nothing was more important than those books, not even food. I am sure my text books would have received better attention than they got, if not for those novels. Fortunately, they did not deter me from passing my exams.

Instead of being time wasters, they awakened my interest in literature. In elementary school, I was rated top of my class in English Language which turned out to be my best subject. In secondary school, I was unbeatable in both English language and English literature. However, as my schoolmates realized how good I was in those subjects it became a disadvantage to me. When the class bullies chose to punish me, they either stole my books or hid them until after the exams.

There was one remarkable incident when one of my classmates stole all my literature books as a way of preventing me from performing better than her. I had to borrow a friend's books to study for the exam. To everyone's surprise, I won the best prize in Literature that year.

I paid a price for my addiction to those beautiful stories. I began to feel like the beautiful princesses who lived in the castles. The stories were so convincing that they turned me into a hopelessly romantic person. I became like one of those beautiful girls in search of their knights in shining armor. A man had to be good looking or he was not worth the trouble. He had to be tall, handsome and with a pointed nose before I could even pay any attention to him. It was when I started reading literature books written by William Shakespeare, Chinua Achebe, Cyprian Ekwensi, Wole Soyinka, Maya Angelou and other famous Authors that my attitude to life started changing. That was when I realized that I should avoid men and women with certain character flaws like addiction to alcohol and cigarettes.

I discovered Desiderata - a great poem that I first read in my early days on campus. Desiderata taught me to avoid loud and aggressive people as well as the importance of contentment. I learned to derive pleasure from every blessing I received and to appreciate inexpensive things. I decided to always strive to be happy.

DESIDERATA
GO PLACIDLY AMID THE NOISE & HASTE
REMEMBER WHAT PEACE THERE MAY BE IN SILENCE
AS FAR AS POSSIBLE WITHOUT SURRENDER, BE ON GOOD
TERMS WITH ALL PERSONS.
SPEAK YOUR TRUTH QUIETLY & CLEARLY, LISTEN TO
OTHERS, EVEN THE DULL AND THE IGNORANT, THEY TOO
HAVE THEIR STORY. AVOID LOUD & AGGRESSIVE PERSONS,
THEY ARE VEXATIOUS TO THE SPIRIT. IF YOU COMPARE
YOURSELF TO OTHERS, YOU MAY BECOME VAIN OR BITTER,
FOR ALWAYS THERE WILL BE GREATER & LESSER PERSONS
THAN YOURSELF. ENJOY YOUR ACHIEVEMENTS AS WELL AS
YOUR PLANS.
KEEP INTERESTED IN YOUR OWN CAREER, HOWEVER
HUMBLE, IT IS A REAL POSSESSION IN THE CHANGING
FORTUNES OF TIME. EXERCISE CAUTION IN YOUR BUSINESS
AFFAIRS, FOR THE WORLD IS FULL OF TRICKERY. BUT LET
THIS NOT BLIND YOU TO WHAT VIRTUE THERE IS.
MANY PERSONS STRIVE FOR HIGH IDEALS & EVERYWHERE
LIFE IS FULL OF HEROISM. BE YOURSELF. ESPECIALLY DO
NOT FEIGN AFFECTION. NEITHER BE CYNICAL ABOUT LOVE,
FOR IN THE FACE OF ALL ARIDITY & DISENCHANTMENT, IT IS
AS PERENNIAL AS THE GRASS. TAKE KINDLY THE COUNSEL
OF THE YEARS, GRACEFULLY SURRENDERING THE THINGS
OF YOUTH. NURTURE STRENGTH OF SPIRIT TO SHIELD YOU IN
SUDDEN MISFORTUNE. BUT DO NOT DISTRESS YOURSELF WITH
DARK IMAGININGS.
MANY FEARS ARE BORN OF FATIGUE AND LONELINESS.
BEYOND A WHOLESOME DISCIPLINE, BE GENTLE WITH
YOURSELF. YOU ARE A CHILD OF THE UNIVERSE, NO LESS
THAN THE TREES & THE STARS, YOU HAVE A RIGHT TO BE
HERE.WHETHER OR NOT IT IS CLEAR TO YOU, NO DOUBT THE

UNIVERSE IS UNFOLDING AS IT SHOULD.

THEREFORE, BE AT PEACE WITH GOD, WHATEVER YOU
CONCEIVE HIM TO BE.

WHATEVER YOUR LABORS & ASPIRATIONS IN THE NOISY
CONFUSION OF LIFE, KEEP PEACE IN YOUR SOUL. WITH ALL
ITS SHAM, DRUDGERY & BROKEN DREAMS, IT IS STILL A
BEAUTIFUL WORLD.

BE CHEERFUL! STRIVE TO BE HAPPY!

WRITTEN BY MAX ERHMANN IN 1927

Gradually, I began to discern that the worst types of men are those that are handsome and vain. Such men are often proud and conceited. They see themselves as God's gift to women. They are the players who cast their nets in wide oceans to entrap women. They enjoy the chase, and believe that the more women they ensnare, the merrier their lives will be. They keep hordes of gullible women at their beck and call, using them as tools to satisfy their selfish interests.

This largely altered the perspective of the kind of man I wanted to associate with. I was more convinced that a woman should look beyond outward appearance. She should be more interested in what is within a man, and that simply means his character. Before getting involved, she should love, understand, and appreciate herself. Self-discovery is very important for every woman and will enable her to understand her strengths, weaknesses, likes and dislikes. A woman needs to know and love herself. If she does not love or understand herself, how can she expect anyone else to love and understand her?

For a woman; character, attitude, and appearance mean everything. While her character and attitude separate her from hordes of other women, her appearance tells you who she really is. A woman of good character comports herself well, even in public. She respects and loves God. She is morally upright.

Due to my personal experience, I have over the years refused to preach early marriage for women. I do not deny that there are benefits of early marriage, one of which is that you have better chances of being alive to enjoy your children. I strongly believe that a woman should first discover herself before connecting with the man that she would share her life with. I still believe that I was too young and naïve when I first got married and that was one of the major reasons it failed. The responsibilities thrust upon women by the marital institution are so much that a woman must be well prepared, physically strong, and mentally ready to perform those duties required of her as a wife and mother.

Women are naturally gullible, and that may explain why drug dealers and fraudsters succeed in ruining the lives of the ones that associate with them. Men with bad addiction, lacking ambition, and focus, distract potentially successful women, turning them into helpless shadows of themselves. Once such men crawl into their lives, they use religion to brainwash them. Caught in the euphoria of love, they forget all their dreams and brilliant plans. The men preach submission and quote the bible upside down. Let me emphasize here that while it is proper for a woman to respect her husband, it is wrong for a woman to allow any man to control her life.

There is a huge difference between submission and control. While submission in this regard, is "… accepting or yielding to a superior force … or authority of another person," control on the other hand means "the power to influence or direct people's behavior or the course of events."

The basic difference is that while submission is a willing act, done out of love and respect; control is enforced due to mental or physical superiority and the person being controlled has no choice. Although it is true that a woman owes it to her husband to submit to him in order to align with his plans, he should not forget that he has also taken the marital vow to love her as Christ loves his church (Ephesians chapter 5, "22 – 30").

It therefore becomes his duty to encourage and provide a suitable environment for her to flourish and be able to achieve her potential. A wise man celebrates his wife's achievements, knowing that if she fails, he too has failed. His wife shares her dreams with him; and he not only encourages her but also helps her to achieve them. Submission does not mean that a woman should forget who she is, sacrifice all her plans and live a miserable and unfulfilled life. A sincere man will tell you, when you dare to ask, that it is better not to have a wife than to have a miserable woman in your household. This was aptly captured by Proverbs 21: 9 –

"It is better to dwell in a corner of the housetop, than with a brawling woman in a wide house."

A woman can only succeed in sparing herself from encounters with destructive men if she knows what to look out for, from the onset. First and foremost, she should understand that character makes a man, not his looks. If she focuses on the heart of the man and not his looks, armed with prayers and guided by the Holy Spirit, she can never go wrong. If she is blessed enough to be found by someone with a strong, positive personality, who has the fear of God, her life will be refreshingly different.

A man, who does not love himself, has no fear of God, despises his mother, and has no respect for his father, can never love a woman. To be found by a God-fearing man, a woman must first love and submit herself to God. Please do not get me wrong. I am not saying here that she can only be found by such a man inside the church. That is a major mistake some women make. While it is indeed possible for him to find her in a church, please note that even devils go to church. They go there on a mission to find and destroy such women who go to church to look for men instead of to worship God. Sometimes, they stumble across some innocent women who mistake them for God fearing men; just because they are church goers.

A good man can be anywhere, but a woman needs God's guidance to be well positioned for such a man to locate her. She should not go looking for him; she should wait to be found. As Maya Angelou aptly puts it, "A woman's heart should be so hidden in Christ that a man should have to seek him first to find her." I completely agree with her. The true nature of a man is so shrouded in mystery and too deep for a woman to unmask. She needs the help of the Holy Spirit.

For male children, it is equally important to start teaching them how to make the right choices as early as possible. Just as female children, everything they have heard or seen affects the decision and choices they later make. The clothes they wear, the books they read, the way the barber cuts their hair and the relationship between their parents all affect their lives.

Unfortunately, some parents believe that because boys do not get pregnant, it is okay to let them run loose until they become adults before they can begin to make choices. This is very wrong. Whether you like it or not, your sons are already choosing what to read, what to listen to, who to hang out with, what to drink and sometimes what to smoke. It is important for you to keep an eye on all their activities and friends and know what they do before it is too late.

Yes, it is true that they cannot get pregnant but they can contact diseases, some of which may haunt them for the rest of their lives. Once they become morally loose, their values will change. Every child should be taught how to identify what is wrong or right from the onset. Some parents believe that boys are unruly and stubborn and they give up on them without making enough effort. They allow their male children to roam about without restriction, boundaries, or rules, until they begin to constitute a nuisance, then they start complaining.

Just like girls, male children should be nurtured and trained while they are still young. They should be made to do their laundry, clean their rooms, and wash plates. They should also learn how to cook. Let parents train and control their children early enough, because that is the only way they can succeed in molding their character, influencing their personality, and transforming them into leaders of tomorrow. They must start when it is still possible to make an impact, otherwise it will be an exercise in futility.

It is very important to start training your child as soon as he is brought home from the hospital. Once he can see or hear, he begins to familiarize himself with his environment. His eyes follow you everywhere you go. He listens to every sound you make and tries to memorize what he hears. He watches and observes. His curious, little eyes follow you around and his tiny ears pick every sound you make. Eventually, he begins to repeat what he heard. This may be why the best possible way to influence a child remains by setting a good example. As a Parent, you must walk your talk. You must not exhibit any trait that you do not want your child to imbibe. Your child should also not get to know that you engaged in such an act, because he may not understand why you insist that he should not do the same.

Do not make the mistake of fooling yourself by thinking that your children will not remember the wrong things you do. If you try to find out, you will be shocked how much your children can remember. A child's brain has such an amazing capacity that by the time he begins to walk, he has already stored up so many memories.

As s a parent, you owe it to your child to make deliberate effort to teach him how to greet, exchange pleasantries and politely make requests by employing the appropriate words. These are words like – "please, may I...."

Teach him how to show appreciation by saying 'thank you.' Teach him how to say 'no,' politely. Teach him how to apologize by saying, 'I am sorry'. Teach him how to be compassionate and how to show empathy. Teach him to sincerely love and demonstrate care for the next person, to enable him overcome selfishness. Deliberately teach him how to make the right choices by purging himself of the 'me first' syndrome. Teach him to understand who he really is – his origins, and to have self-value. Teach him the basic principles of life. Teach him how to pray, love, and appreciate God. Teach him how to set goals for himself and set a definite purpose for his life. Teach him how to focus on his goals and how to strive to achieve them. Help him to formulate good character while he is still young.

When I look around me, I see lots of lost children, wasting away, comporting themselves in an appalling manner. Their obvious lack of virtue and values is very disturbing. I see how confused and ignorant they have become. Clad in indecent clothing, they are like sheep without a shepherd. They parade the streets freely clad in spaghetti strap tops, half shoulder tops, miniskirts, bum shorts, halter neck tops, crop tops, and mini dresses.

Boys prefer to wear trousers with loose or no belts. Their trousers drop halfway, revealing filthy boxer shorts. They drag their feet around with an obvious nonchalant attitude like zombies, with bushy or crazy haircuts and red eyes indicating insufficient sleep. Their slurred speech is proof of indulgence in alcohol or hard drugs. Earphones block their ears that were meant for hearing, even while crossing the road. They are like an ignorant flock of sheep rushing towards the slaughter house, without even realizing it. As bad as it seems, the situation can still get worse unless they are taught how to make the right choices. Knowing how to survive peer pressure really helps.

If you determine to always do the right thing, no matter what is at stake, you begin to find yourself making the right choices. First, acknowledge God, and then release yourself to the guidance of the Holy Spirit. Pray ceaselessly and do not base your choices on your feelings or selfish preferences. The two factors necessary for making the right choices are a positive mental attitude and the right motive.

> "YOU HAVE A CHOICE, LIVE, OR DIE. EVERY BREATH IS A CHOICE. EVERY MINUTE IS A CHOICE. EVERY TIME YOU DON'T THROW YOURSELF DOWN THE STAIRS, THAT'S A CHOICE. EVERY TIME YOU DON'T CRASH YOUR CAR, YOU RE -ENLIST"
>   – CHUCK PALAHNIUK

LESSONS:

- Make friends with those you can either learn from or influence
- No other person can determine the path your life takes but you
- Be observant
- Reading can be both instructive and fun
- What you read affects your character
- Character makes a man, not his looks
- A woman should discover herself before marriage
- Control is different from submission
- A wise man celebrates his wife's achievements knowing that if she fails, he too has failed
- It is better not to have a wife than to have a miserable woman in your household
- A man who does not love himself, has no fear of God, despises his mother, and has no respect for his father can never love a woman
- To be found by a God-fearing man, a woman must first seek God
- Strive to be happy

CHAPTER 3

BE HONEST

> **"AN HONEST MAN IS RESPECTED BY ALL PARTIES" –**
> **WILLIAM HAZLITT**

The only way for anyone to remain upright is through a personal conviction and fear of God. When someone is convinced that he is doing the right thing, it is more difficult to influence him in a negative manner than when he is in doubt. If you have properly groomed and trained your child, teaching him what is right and wrong, he will most likely decide to be upright. By the age of 10, he is already armed with all he needs to know about God. He will already have developed good manners. In addition, he will be obedient and will respect his parents, teachers, and neighbors. He will also respect people in authority. He will understand that the world does not belong to him and everyone is not at his beck and call. He will also understand that boundaries exist and that there are rules he is expected to obey.

As he grows into adulthood, he begins to have a change of mind to drop his childhood exuberance and tendencies and start taking responsibility for his actions. This change of heart comes with maturity and should be done willingly. When someone chooses to be honest and well behaved, when temptation comes his way, he will always remember that he made the choice to be upright. In a world full of radicalism and immorality, it is increasingly more difficult to be upright. It can only happen with personal conviction.

Uprightness was one of the noble principles I imbibed from my late father who strongly believed in keeping his hands clean. Recognizing that one day he would stand before God to give an account of his life on earth, being upright was very important to him. In his relationship with other people, he remained honest until his death. His decision made him lose so much in terms of riches and wealth that he had every opportunity to accumulate. He died a noble and uncontaminated man.

It was while I was in secondary school that I first witnessed the satisfaction and joy that comes with rejecting evil. My father was wooed by a group of fraudulent men who were forging our national currency, Nigerian Naira. He found the strength to refuse to join them. It must have been difficult for him. My father had nine children to feed and train and really needed money. Months later the men were arrested by the police. It was when I saw the publication on the front page of our national newspaper that I understood how our lives would have been affected if my father had succumbed to the temptation.

He won my heart on that day and became my mentor. Years later, I was at a burial ceremony where I met a man who worked with my father. I was delighted when he spoke about my father in a very positive way to members of our group. The moment I was introduced he took a keen interest in me. He said to me -

"Your father is a good man. I am not saying it because you are here. He is one of the few good men. Tell him that you met me and that I said so."

He talked about the years they worked together and how my father refused to cheat anyone or be involved in any corrupt practice. He expressed so much respect and admiration for my father that I stood six feet taller among the crowd. It is true that when you are straight forward, sincere, and honest, people may not like you and you may even have fewer friends but do not let this bother you because it will only be for a while. The moment they realize that you can be trusted; they begin to accept you for who are and associate more with you.

In relationships, honesty always pays. Lies can be very damaging and will always be revealed. When you start lying, be prepared to tell more lies. Lies beget more lies. There is everything good about being honest because it is easier to tell the truth than it is to lie. Lying takes a lot of effort. You must spend time thinking before you can even construct the lie. Then you need to ensure that it is believable and are prepared to answer the questions that will follow.

Instead of lying or trying to cover up your situation, it is always better to explain how things really are. Be truthful and transparent because you never know who can help make your situation better. Although lying has become very fashionable, especially among the younger generation, everyone appreciates honesty. You feel encouraged, loved, and appreciated if you are hearing the truth. It is important to always speak the truth.

My late father trusted me so much because he knew that I would always tell him the truth, no matter the situation. When I and my siblings moved away from home, he relied so much on me to confirm what was going on with us. Whenever we disagreed or quarreled and he was not sure of whatever report was given to him, he would request to speak with me. He knew that I would always tell him the truth, even when I was partly to blame and he often said so. Can you imagine being singled out by your father as the one person he could trust amongst your siblings? I can assure you that it is such a difficult position because you will always be attacked by all your siblings.

That was my plight, but I continued to tell the truth. Eventually, my siblings all began to trust and confide in me. I have always been there for them whenever they needed to hear the truth. They came to realize that they could always rely on me for sincere advice at any time. I played a similar role amongst my friends and in places where I worked. Speaking the truth will place you on a pedestal among your peers and make others look up to you for direction. Wherever I find myself, I see people in search of solutions to their problems approaching me for counseling. They eagerly share their experiences with me. It is always exciting to see their faces light up with the realization of facing up to the truth, no matter how difficult it may seem.

Raising children who are honest and who appreciate honesty should be every parent's priority. This requires parents to be honest. Children do not just practice what they are told but emulate what they see their parents do. When your child starts telling lies, you should be worried unless you are also a lying parent. Children who grow to become thieves start by telling lies. Good deceivers evolve to become criminals. If you notice that your child is lying, do all you can to stop him from doing so. Teach him the importance of being honest.

Years back, when Adaora, my daughter was still a child. Then, she was only six years old. I employed a nanny to take care of her. Lily, was a young girl that my mother found and sent to me to become my nanny. My mother knew nothing about the girl except that her parents were said to be good people. Within a few months of living with us, I noticed some unusual occurrences around the house. There were days

You Too Can Overcome Life's Challenges

I returned from work to find the door to my room unlocked, although I was sure that I locked it before leaving home. Drawn curtains were sometime pulled aside, while my toiletries were out of place. I was sure no one had a spare key to my room and therefore confident that I was being unnecessarily finicky. One day, I noticed that the cover of my body cream was broken; I asked Lily if any one entered my room in my absence and she quickly said "No ma." I brushed off the ill feeling.

Lily was a sweet young girl with an angelic face. Although I had seen traces of disobedience in her, I had no idea how far she could go until the day I was cooking with my younger sister, Chizo. It was Adaora's birthday and we were having a party. We left the kitchen for some minutes and were shocked to discover that the full bucket of deliciously fried chicken which we left behind had been reduced to three quarter of the bucket. We were surprised but could not figure out what happened to the chicken. Lily quickly denied tampering with the chicken. It was the day she fought with our security man that I realized where the chicken went. Apparently, she had been feeding him from my kitchen in exchange for his attention and friendship. Lily's habit of lying reached a crescendo on the day the keys to my house went missing. I came home that night and found Adaora and her sitting outside the door. Adaora, who was still wearing her school uniform ran to me, apologizing for having lost the key to our house. Instantly, I knew who set her up to tell such lies about a set of keys that was not even in her care. I was so furious that I snapped. I landed a sharp slap on Lily's cheek and demanded to know the truth. They both fell on their knees and started confessing.

The real story was that Lily lost the keys on her way from picking Adaora up from school and convinced her to lie to me, thinking it would spare her from my wrath. She did not know that teaching Adaora to tell lies was an offence much worse than misplacing my house keys. All along, Adaora had been groomed to always speak the truth and I was not prepared to allow someone convert her to a liar. Also, I knew that anyone who could lie so well and so convincingly would make a good thief.

I therefore wrote to my mum and arranged for my sister to travel down to the East with her. I did not want to wait for her to turn Adaora into a lying little girl. On the day they were leaving, I allowed Lily to pack her bags into my car before I announced my intention to search them. She became very uncomfortable. The next thing I saw was Lily grabbing her bag and running to the back of the house and we all ran in hot pursuit of her. When we caught up with her, her loot was strewn all over the ground where it fell. They were quite an eye full.

We saw children's clothes, toys, wrist watches and some other items purchased with the money she pilfered from me but there was no money. We decided to search further. That was when we found the money she stole. They were in local and foreign currency. The money was wrapped up in a handkerchief at the bottom of her bag. Apparently, she had been stealing since she arrived and stockpiling her loot in a vacant apartment in our block which was still under construction. Adaora was so shocked that she stood there, saying repeatedly;

Lily, so you are a thief.

Lily was a kleptomaniac. She did not just steal from me, but also from my neighbor who traded in children's clothes and other neighbors whose homes she visited. What she did was a huge embarrassment for me. I had to go knocking on doors to return the stolen items to some of my neighbors that I had never interacted with. Unfortunately, Lily was unstoppable. In her determination to be a celebrated thief, she stole from a female commuter that travelled with them to Enugu.

When the woman started looking for her purse, my sister noticed that Lily was sitting rather subdued in one corner. She told the bus driver to search her. The search produced nothing. It was after she was returned to her parents' house, her father was so angry that he decided to strip her naked and search her. The woman's wallet fell off her panties. He dragged her, kicking and whining, back to my mother with the stolen wallet. By then, the woman had continued her journey with a very painful heart. She was a widow on her way to her village for Christmas celebrations. All her savings was in that purse.

Lily's father was so embarrassed and disappointed with his daughter that he confessed that he sent her away from home, because he was hoping that she could stop stealing. He said that she was a disgrace to his family. She was caught stealing from their neighbors several times and from their church offering basket. My mother advised him to drop the widow's wallet inside an offering basket in their church.

Dishonesty means cheating other people. When you are a cheat, you hurt yourself and every person around you. You lose credibility and no one believes or trusts you. If you want to be happy, start by being honest. Also, settle your bills. Do not wait until people you owe begin to chase you around. Learn how to keep your promises. When you give your word, keep it. When you borrow, pay back, on or before the due date.

> "NO LEGACY IS SO RICH AS HONESTY"
> – WILLIAM SHAKESPEARE

LESSONS:

- A child should be properly home trained before the age of ten
- Change of heart from childhood truancy to responsible adulthood is a deliberate act
- Personal conviction and fear of God are what will help you to maintain uprightness.
- Say no to evil
- If you want to be respected, be honest
- Honesty always pays
- It is easier to tell the truth than to tell lies
- Everyone appreciates honesty
- Speaking the truth will place you on a pedestal
- Raising children to be sincere and to appreciate honesty should be every parent's priority
- Children who grow to become thieves start by lying
- You do not solve your problems by running away from them
- If you want to be happy, start by being honest

CHAPTER 4

DEVELOP A POSITIVE MENTAL ATTITUDE

> "NOTHING CAN STOP THE MAN WITH THE RIGHT MENTAL ATTITUDE FROM ACHIEVING HIS GOAL, NOTHING ON EARTH CAN HELP THE MAN WITH THE WRONG MENTAL ATTITUDE"
> – W.W. ZIEGE

Developing a positive mental attitude is a first step to becoming a successful person. You should first and foremost be able to visualize whatever you want to achieve, before you even begin to go after it. When you believe that it is achievable, only then can you make the necessary effort to succeed. If you start entertaining fear and believing that your plans may not work, the more chances that you will become complacent which often leads to failure. The world is so full of disenchantment and pessimism.

Every day we listen to news relating to crime, war and death caused by natural disasters. Terrorism and radicalism have also taken another dimension. Aside from those, currency devaluation and fear of inflation are enough to deter any would have been successful entrepreneur from going into business. What makes the difference between you and every other person is developing a positive mental attitude. If you do not develop a positive mental attitude, you will give in to despondency, misery, lamentation, and helplessness.

In the face of the numerous challenges that I faced, I never stopped being positive. My attitude was what kept me stable enough to work out solutions to my challenges. Maintaining a strong faith in God and recognizing that there will always be a way out of every difficult situation kept me going. Even as a single mother, I remained strong and positive. Instead of focusing on my problems, I continued to concentrate on finding solutions.

You Too Can Overcome Life's Challenges

A positive attitude will influence your approach to the challenges you may be facing and will determine how much effort you make to combat them. It will also determine how persistent you will be when it seems your efforts are not yielding the expected result. Developing a positive mental attitude at an early age will not only help you to dream big dreams but also assist you in striving to achieve them. When your plans fail, a positive attitude will make you see a ray of sunshine at the end of the black tunnel. It will help you to come up with other strategies to revive your vision and keep you striving until you achieve your goals. A positive mental attitude keeps you calm even in the face of turmoil; it keeps you focused and continues to motivate you.

Believing that you have all it takes to achieve your goal, will make you bold enough to push towards success. A defeatist attitude has never and will never be an advantage to anyone. It only leads to failure. Most times, people that fail in their endeavors already fail, even before they try. Those who dare to achieve, believe that they can and that is what makes them keep trying, even when they fail. Determined, they persist until the bright light in the horizon becomes a reality. More than any other thing, the confidence that they can, remains the key factor for their success. To succeed, you must set definite goals. A positive attitude energizes and propels you towards achieving your goals, while a negative attitude undermines your efforts.

If you believe in yourself, you are most likely to succeed in whatever you set out to do. If you entertain doubts, you have already failed, even before you start. The greatest reasons for failing are fear and self-doubt. Having faith in God helps you develop a can-do attitude. This attitude will show in everything you do, especially in the way you approach your goals. It will affect your personality. You will have self-control. You will be able to control your mind and body, while making effort to achieve your goals.

To succeed, you need to be able to meditate, review, and imbibe a change of attitude. You cannot move from one level to another with the same attitude. It is only a positive attitude that will help you achieve your aim. With a negative attitude, you unknowingly magnify the obstacles that exist, imagine the ones that do not and continue to limit yourself. There will always be obstacles. The right attitude is a positive one and that is the attitude of successful individuals who keep pushing until the locked doors cave in. You can be successful if you try but you really must get out of your comfort zone. People who do not dare to achieve success never will.

> "ABILITY IS WHAT YOU'RE CAPABLE OF DOING. MOTIVATION DETERMINES WHAT YOU DO. ATTITUDE DETERMINES HOW WELL YOU DO IT"
> – LOU HOLTZ

LESSONS:

- Developing a positive mental attitude is a first step to success
- Entertaining fear is the beginning of failure
- A positive mental attitude influences your effort and determines your result
  There is always a light at the end of every dark tunnel
  A defeatist attitude has never been an advantage to anyone
  To succeed, you need a change of attitude
  If you want to succeed, get out of your comfort zone

CHAPTER 5

CULTIVATE THE RIGHT MOTIVE

"OUR SOULS MAY LOSE THEIR PEACE AND EVEN DISTURB OTHER PEOPLE'S IF WE ARE ALWAYS CRITICIZING TRIVIAL ACTIONS – WHICH OFTEN ARE NOT REAL DEFECTS AT ALL, BUT WE CONSTRUE THEM WRONGLY THROUGH OUR IGNORANCE OF THEIR MOTIVES."
– SAINT TERESA OF AVILA

As you mature and begin to chart a course for your life, it is important that you always think about your actions. Having the right motive for your actions will help in your character formation. Let what is driving you towards the actions you take be the right reason. If your motive is right, then you cannot go wrong and will not be on the wrong side of the law. God knows your motives even when others do not. When the motive is right, most often than not, we get what we desire. When you pray with the right motive, God answers. When your motive is to acquire items, you may not need, just to show off or oppress others, you may not get them. Even when you get them, you will not be satisfied. When your motive is to oppress, intimidate and destroy others, whatever you acquire or achieve will never make you happy.

Always be mindful of your motive. Before you make a choice, consider your motive. Some ladies buy too many clothes they do not need, decorate their wardrobes with them and never get to wear them. The clothes rot away until they realize that they have wasted funds that could have been used for better projects. I was guilty of buying clothes, shoes and bags on impulse until I had to call myself to order.

Showing off has become part of the culture in some countries. In a situation where you see someone who can barely afford to feed his family decorating the grounds of his rented apartment with expensive cars to show off to his neighbors, he is sowing seeds of sorrow. If he saved up the money, he would have upgraded himself to acquiring a property of his own. He would have been living in his own house. He would probably have rented part of it and be earning some return on his investment, instead of spending money on maintaining his fleet of vehicles. He may eventually end up borrowing from the same neighbor he was trying so hard to impress. Before you take any action, learn how to pause, and ask yourself what drives you. If your motive is wrong, it is time to make a change.

If your motive is right, stay on course. Eventually, people that misunderstood you will change their opinion. In every action I took, I deliberately considered my motive. It made me stand out from the crowd. Although I was largely misunderstood, my reasons always charted my course. Eventually, my destination became clearer to others, after my purpose had been achieved.

I left Lagos, Nigeria on a journey that would completely change my life. Adaora, my daughter gained admission to study Biological Sciences at a University in Accra. She was only sixteen years old and I was on a mission to Accra, Ghana to help her get adapted to her new environment. I was a single parent. I had single handedly nurtured Adaora from age one and half years old to sixteen. It was after visiting her in school and finding out that she was the youngest in her class that I made the decision to move to Accra. I watched in fear as other students teased her when they realized her age. One of her roommates candidly advised her to return to secondary school. She added that her sister who was Adaora's age mate was still in secondary school. I still remember the girl's name, Valentina and these were her exact words –

She is like my younger sister who is still in secondary school. She is too young to be here.

Valentina was addressing me and urging me to take my daughter home.

Although Adaora laughed it off, I became worried. I knew right there and then that I needed to do something about her situation. I was very much aware of so many children who were sent abroad to study by their parents and who became victims of peer pressure because there was no family member to guide them. Influenced by what they saw around them, they experimented with drugs and embraced all sorts of immoral adventures. Please do not get me wrong. It was not that I did not trust my daughter. I had groomed her thoroughly from an early age to be prim and proper. I knew that she could clearly differentiate between right and wrong. She also had a clear idea of what my expectations were. Unlike many of her age mates who studied in mixed secondary schools, she was able to avoid succumbing to pressure from male students.

Adaora comported herself so well that she became a point of reference for parents who were trying to save their children from falling astray. I once had a good laugh over an incident that occurred during her secondary school days when some female students faced punishment for partying with the boys. They were caught dancing and merry making all night when they were supposed to have been sleeping. As Adaora narrated the story, my anxiety got the better of me and I quickly interrupted:

I hope you were not one of them.

I cannot even begin to describe the astonished look on her face when she responded –

Mummy, you think I do not know you. You will just kill me.

It was my turn to stare at her in shock as she continued:

When I was thinking of how to make 99.9%? How could I possibly have time for partying?

Although I was a bit worried about such an unusual outburst from my daughter, she said it with so much love and understanding that I simply recognized that my parenting job was successful.

The first step was for me to go over there and spend some time. This was to enable me understand Ghanaians and their culture. Next, I set out on a mission to secure a job before making the quantum leap. Some of my friends and family tried their best to discourage me but I was adamant. As one of my former colleagues who relocated to the United States after she got married wrote in an e mail to me:

We thought you had gone crazy when you folded up your palace in Lagos and moved to Ghana.

She was right. I had a good job and was living in a very comfortable home. It was a three-bedroom duplex in Lagos. Each room had ensuite bathroom. I had everything I needed for a good life but my daughter was much more important than all that I left behind. I knew that if anything happened to her because of the distance between Ghana and Nigeria, I could never forgive myself. I had to make the required sacrifice. I left my comfortable home and moved into a one room apartment in Accra until I made enough money to do better. Family always comes first. I believe that there is no sacrifice made for someone's child that can ever be too much. That was one of the lessons I learned from my parents at a very tender age, which I will always remember.

My parents gave me so much love and I had to do the same for my daughter. My mother always ran to our side, no matter where we were, once she heard that we were in distress. My father either came along or encouraged her. As we developed and matured, we knew that they were always there for us. That solid family support meant so much to us. My mother supported us with constant prayers, thereby shielding us from numerous calamities. Every parent should always try to be there for their child. A parent's support goes a long way in shaping a child's future.

Adaora was going through a very trying period in her life. She was battling to get into the medical school. I was right there by her side. Her ambition was high, the sacrifice was huge, but it was worth it. By the time I became a manager in an advertising company in Accra, I moved into a more comfortable apartment. I never regretted leaving Lagos. Eventually, it became obvious that my decision was right. All those who chided me turned around to applaud my sacrifice.

Learn how not to be anxious for an applause in the beginning. It is better to wait until the end, then, it will be louder.

> "NEVER JUDGE A MAN'S ACTION UNTIL YOU KNOW HIS MOTIVES"
> – VIKAS SWARUP

LESSONS:

- Your motive determines your success rate
- Ensure your motive is right
- Let your motive chart your course
- The right motive yields treasures, while the wrong motive sows' sorrows
- Prioritize your life
- Make the necessary sacrifice for your family
- A parent's support goes a long way in shaping his child's future
- Family always comes first
- Let the applause come after you have achieved your aim
- If you follow the rhythm of your heart, you can never go wrong

CHAPTER 6

BE VIGILANT

> "HE IS MOST FREE FROM DANGER, WHO, EVEN WHEN SAFE,
> IS ON HIS GUARD" – PABILIUS SYRUS

There is always a lesson to learn from everything we see or experience. There is much to gain from being vigilant. You learn a lot from observing people and animals and taking time out to study your environment. Studying the environment will teach you how man relates to his environment. You will understand man's relationship with the animals in his territory and the relationship between the animals themselves.

Over the years, observing human behavior helped me a great deal to understand and better appreciate other people. It also helped me to appreciate their manner of reasoning and motives. Man is a social and political animal. Someone who is hungry can only think of where his next meal will come from, while a person that has been hurt will naturally be concerned with either pursuing justice or vengeance.

While a happy man will be disposed to being kind to the next person, a disgruntled man will be too busy complaining and lamenting to bother about making someone else happy. Attitudes, reactions, and responses differ from one individual to another. Understanding how each person feels and knowing exactly what to expect from him, can reduce his ability to surprise or shock you.

In business, it is always helpful to be guided by a sound knowledge of your environment and the behavioral patterns of the people that share it with you. This will help you in plotting your business strategies. If you formulate your strategies with such considerations, you can hardly go wrong. Aside from the advantage of the knowledge acquired in taking time out to watch and study people around you and your environment, being vigilant helps you to relax. You know exactly what is happening around you. It helps you to feel safe and secure. It keeps you away from danger. Many people fall victims of circumstances due to being absent minded. They get carried away by either their gadgets or events happening around them. There are so many distractions in the world today, but we must try to remain present in the moment. It is only when you are alert that you can objectively determine your next move and it will be to your advantage.

You can tell if you are being followed by a would-be kidnapper, if you are alert. If someone is about to rob you, you may be able to escape when you are alert. Dangerous people can tell when you are alert. They watch you for a while before they pounce on you. They know that it is easier to succeed with someone that is distracted. When you are in public, form the habit of keeping your phone out of sight until it rings. The cell phone is a huge distraction. When you pick it up to take a call, keep your eyes open, scanning your environment as you take that call. Keep your conversation short and call the person back once you are alone. Remember that the person that called you does not want you to get hurt, kidnapped, or killed. There is nothing that is so important that will warrant your answering the phone when your life is in danger. Your life is more important. If you are in a cab, watch the road like you are the one on the wheel. Do not take chances. If you sleep off, it may be your last ride.

Keep your phone close to you in case you need it. You may need to dial 911 to save your life. Remember that your phone can also save your life. Learn not to trust anyone when you are travelling alone. You may be the reason someone else is on board and you may never know until it is too late. If you are observant, you will anticipate events before they occur and you will be better prepared to handle them. This involves listening to every sound around you whether you are being addressed or not. If you are not sure of what is being said, ask questions. You can never go wrong with asking questions. Seek clarifications and situations will become clearer to you.

LESSONS:

- Being vigilant protects you from danger
- If you are alert, you can anticipate events before they occur
- Dangerous people can tell if you are alert or not

CHAPTER 7

PEOPLE WATCH

> "EVER SINCE HE COULD REMEMBER, HE'D PEOPLE –
> WATCHED TO PASS TIME. WHEN HE WAS YOUNGER,
> EVERYONE TOLD HIM IT WAS RUDE. HE HADN'T STOPPED,
> MERELY PERFECTED HIS TECHNIQUE"
> – LAURA OLIVIA

It is as simple as the name implies and means watching people. It involves critically observing my fellow men and women in their various situations to understand them better. This simple hobby of mine helps me to anticipate human behavior and makes it possible for me to determine how people react in a certain situation and how differently they will respond if the situation changes. Wherever I find myself; on the road, at the airport, in the office, at a conference or even while attending an event, I observe and study everyone around me. I do this without their even knowing that they are being watched.

I know that you are probably thinking, why not? After all, she is a writer. Let me explain that I got into this habit not because of my writing but simply out of curiosity. I started watching people, long before I even began to write. I guess it was because I preferred knowing and understanding whatever was happening around me in order not to be taken unaware. I hate unpleasant surprises. Studying other people helps me a great deal in understanding behavioral peculiarities of individuals. Interestingly, I have discovered that behavioral patterns differ from age to age and from culture to culture.

Several factors determine the character traits of people. It could be their gender, age or their climate conditions. I have come to realize that while a grandmother shouts and yells on the phone while having a simple conversation with her daughter, a teenager holds a similar conversation without the next person hearing a word of what he is saying. This will most likely be because of the age difference and the fact that the teenager's ears function better. He hears what is being said to him easily and therefore does not feel the need to shout to be understood. I also learned that a husband and wife can communicate effectively without words. Just by looking at each other or one of them placing his or her head on the other person's shoulders, a lot is said and understood.

When a man is holding his wife's hand, he is communicating. I have also discovered that there are different kinds of hugs and kisses and different ways of saying either yes or no. This can be done through body movements or postures, without a word being uttered. This may be the reason why it is possible for someone to be saying something while his body language is conveying a very different message. For you to understand him, you will have to interpret both his body language as well as his spoken words.

The main reason why citizens of Europe, America, and other cold climate regions drink lots of tea and coffee is because of the cold weather. This is probably the same reason why they are more romantic than Africans and others that live in hot climate. They feel greater need for close physical contact with their loved ones for warmth against the cold climate.

From watching People, I learned that the way people perceive situations differ. They also react in different ways to similar situations, depending on their culture, perception, educational and social background, as well as level of exposure. You will be amazed at how much you can learn for free just from watching people.

> "TO ASSIST THE QUALITY OF THOUGHTS OF PEOPLE, DON'T LISTEN TO THEIR WORDS, BUT WATCH THEIR ACTIONS."
> – AMIT KALANTRI

LESSONS:

- Attitudes, reactions, and responses differ from one individual to another
- Observe people to understand them
- Watching people helps you to relax
- Being observant helps you to anticipate human behavior and avoid surprises

CHAPTER 8

NATURE WATCH

"THOSE WHO CONTEMPLATE THE BEAUTY OF THE EARTH
FIND RESERVES OF STRENGTH THAT WILL ENDURE AS
LONG AS LIFE LASTS... THERE IS SOMETHING INFINITELY
HEALING IN THE REPEATED REFRAINS OF NATURE – THE
ASSURANCE THAT DAWN COMES AFTER NIGHT,
AND SPRING AFTER WINTER."
– RACHEL CARSON, SILENT SPRING

Nature watch is man's way of appreciating God in the most amazing way. Start by looking around you. What do you see? You will see flowers, trees, birds, animals, the sun, sea and the sky. You will see everything that God has created for us to derive pleasure from. Back in my university days, I formed the habit of strolling on campus in the evenings with a very close friend of mine.

Joy and I went on what we simply labeled 'Moon watching.' Joy had an artistic mind, just as I did, and we found out that we enjoyed spending time together, appreciating what God freely gave to humanity. We loved to stroll around the campus in the evenings; early enough to catch the sun setting and watch the stars begin to emerge from behind the clouds. We walked around, counting the stars, while looking out for the moon. This was in the 80s and we could easily have been misunderstood, but I was dating someone who was matured enough to understand what I meant by 'Nature watch' when I explained the reason for my evening stroll with a fellow woman.

One day, he came looking for me and was told by one of my roommates that I went for a stroll with Joy. He waited outside in the cold, until we returned and wanted to know why I went out strolling with someone else instead of him. Fortunately, he was a patient kind of man - the type that would demand for an explanation instead of strutting off in anger, having jumped to the wrong conclusions. That was the day he found out about my love for nature and we started taking walks together.

Roaming around my school premises, opened my eyes to a whole lot. I began to appreciate the beauty of nature. I realized that there are so many types of stars in the universe. In a short while, I was able to identify the one that became my most favorite, the shooting star. The sight of a shooting star (which I later realized was a visible path of a meteoroid as it entered the atmosphere) always delighted me in a special way. This was probably because of its shape, captivating beauty, and speed. As far as I was concerned, the shooting star was one of the stars. I had no idea then that it was a falling star, descending onto earth. It was so breathtakingly beautiful, leaving me captivated, each night that I saw it. I was not good in Geography and up until today still stumble through finding my way around, which is part of the reason that I do not enjoy driving. However, I derive an absolute joy in admiring the abundant beauty in my natural surroundings.

I also became aware of the different shades the sun assumed, especially when it was about to set. Those were my most delightful moments – to gaze at the sun as it set. As soon as I could afford a camera, I bought one for taking many pictures of the setting sun. Although I have no idea where the photographs are today, I still remember the wholesome joy I derived from admiring the pictures, repeatedly - a memory that will remain with me forever. They were so beautiful. There is an inner peace that comes from admiring nature and I always felt so relaxed after such walks. You too can learn to relax by taking walks. It is also a great opportunity to think, if you can find a quiet and peaceful garden or park to stroll.

During my National Service Year in Calabar, I took trips to Oron and its environment. That was when I discovered the sea and its peculiar beauty. It was then that I wrote a poem about the sea – 'To Thee Great Sea' which was written during one of my trips to the hinterland. The poem was one of those published in my first collection of poems - Panorama.

You Too Can Overcome Life's Challenges

To Thee Great Sea
Oh, great sea
So calm and
Yet so wild
Nature, thou art beautiful
And your mystery surpasses
The wisdom of ages

We, the living enjoy thy wondrous gifts
But cannot explain them
The hills, the valleys, and the trees
All are part of thee
But thee, mysterious, beautiful sea
Lies above the understanding
Of we mortals

When I moved to Lagos, I discovered the Bar Beach and began to visit it at weekends. I spent time sitting and watching the sea pass me by. I relished savoring the scent of fresh or polluted air emanating from the water, whilst watching the changing patterns of the waves. I must confess that I gathered a lot of inspiration from the sea and its changing moods. Unfortunately, I never really learned how to swim, a fact I still regret up until this very day. I had no opportunity until I became an undergraduate. When I decided to learn how to swim, I bought a swimsuit and went over to the pool in my university campus. I was young, beautiful, but not very adventurous.

While waiting for my turn to be coached, I stood by the pool, watching other learners. That was when I noticed that the coach was much more interested in fondling the girls than teaching them how to swim. He was handsome with a well-built body. His groomed biceps were quite visible, inside, and out of the water. He played with some of the girls and they giggled in excitement, while diving in and out of the water. They laughed and cheered each other as the supposed swimming lessons went on. Soon, it was my turn. I quickly considered whether to ignore what I witnessed and go into the water. Was I to go ahead and trade my dignity for swimming lessons or take a walk out of the pool area? When the coach turned and beckoned unto me, I saw the glint of lustful anticipation in his eyes and decided not to give him the satisfaction of fondling me in that water.

He and the other girls were surprised when they saw me spin around and walk out of the pool area without a word, holding my head high with every dignity I could gather. That was how I missed a golden opportunity of learning how to swim. Much as I never regretted the decision I took on that day, I really wish the situation could have been different.

I owe my nature watching habit to my late father because he inspired me to appreciate nature. He used to take me and my siblings around our gardens and beyond. He taught us names of everything we could see; from flowers to anthills, animals, birds, and fruits. He never realized how much he prepared me for appreciating life and the gifts freely given to humanity by God. I learned from him that there is a whole lot we can teach our children. I got into the habit of commenting on the things I saw, while admiring my surroundings. Adaora, my daughter would react by admonishing me, "Mummy, you have started again." Instead of getting offended, it always made me smile, because then I knew that despite her obvious cynicism, she was learning something new.

From being vigilant, I learned how to differentiate between men and animals, and acknowledge their similarities. I therefore became better able to identify the genuineness or otherwise of someone's affectionate display, just by looking into their eyes. Sometimes, I recognize pretense, and see through hypocrisy, which makes my skin crawl. I can distinguish between genuine laughter and a pretentious one, often delivered with a false note.

There is a huge difference between that laughter, the one that has a ring of truth in it, spiced with cheerfulness and the 'well, let's just get along kind of laughter.' Being in tune with nature ensures that I am never lonely. Sometimes, I talk to myself, crack jokes, and laugh at my own jokes. On the down side, where others may have endured out of ignorance, I sometimes react too soon; appreciating when someone is being sincere to me and detesting when he or she is lying. Sometimes, I caution my natural instincts and endure until it is time to let go. The advantage is that I can determine how much of the deceit I can accommodate and plan my exit from the relationship in such a manner that the repercussion is often minimized.

I therefore recommend that as a parent, you should consider it part of your duty to teach your children how to appreciate their environment. It will help them understand nature; appreciate God's favor to man and relish the beauty of our world. It is absolutely an amazing world that we live in. By teaching your children how to enjoy the simple things that life has to offer, they will be better positioned to value complex and luxurious items.

Teach them how to laugh at mundane situations, so that they can enjoy their lives and avoid growing old and wrinkled, too soon. If they do not smile enough, they may end up with deep worry lines on their faces and spend their later years lamenting on how much time they wasted, pursuing unimportant things instead of finding time to relax.

I have often heard elderly people lamenting that if they knew better, they would have used the time they deployed in pursuing wealth for making themselves and people around them happy. That makes a lot of sense to me because in today's fast paced and crazy world, if you do not create time for happiness, by the time you are old, you will be lucky if you can find anyone interested in listening to your tales of woe. Our children are so busy with their phones and tablets to have time for a simple conversation, even with their aging parents.

It is better to start enjoying the free gifts of life that are available to you while you are still young because that is all you can hold on to when you are old and retired from the hustle and bustle of life. These days, children have forgotten how to appreciate kindness; they no longer know how to say hello, thank you, please, may I, I am sorry and all those wonderful words that calm nerves. They spend all their time wrapped up in their gadgets and social media. They are mostly lonely and unhappy children.

This may be why the number of young people with mental health issues and those committing suicide has been on the increase. Elderly people often find themselves abandoned and are only consoled by the quality of lives they have already lived. The duty therefore lies on all parents to deliberately teach their children how best to find true joy and fulfillment by truly appreciating the natural gifts that Mother Earth has freely given to us.

> "I FELT MY LUNGS INFLATE WITH THE ONRUSH OF SCENERY
> – AIR, MOUNTAINS, TREES, PEOPLE. I THOUGHT, THIS IS
> WHAT IT IS TO BE HAPPY."
>   – SYLVIA PLATH

LESSONS:

- Admiring nature gives one inner peace and joy in a turbulent world
- Walking is a therapy. Learn to relax by taking walks
- Nothing comes free, there is always a price to pay
- Hold on to your dignity, it is all you have
- If you want to know how genuine someone is, look into his eyes
- Gadgets do not bring true happiness
- There is an inner peace that comes from admiring nature
- Find time to relax

CHAPTER 9

TRUST AND APPRECIATE GOD

"BLESSED IS THE MAN WHO TRUSTS IN THE LORD WHOSE CONFIDENCE IS IN HIM" – JEREMIAH 17: 7

If you really want to be successful, you must acknowledge God. You must trust and appreciate him for all he has been doing for you. Remember that the world is mysterious and the heart of man is said to be innately wicked. We need God's guidance, protection, and assistance throughout our earthly journey. If you trust him, he will open doors for you and make what seems impossible become achievable. In whatever situation you find yourself, believe in God, and trust him. If you appreciate him for everything, he has done for you, then you are guaranteed that he will do more. If you acknowledge that you did not come to the world by some accident and that God is always there to see you through challenges, then you should begin to trust him. Nothing is impossible for God. If you sincerely desire what you are aspiring for, pray diligently, while working towards it and it will be yours.

Some people pray tirelessly and get no result because they do not trust God. Trust God and he will answer you. I have often received, because I trusted. God wants us to come to him as little children to their father. He wants us to see him as our father and totally believe that he can fulfill all our needs.

I had a horrifying experience some years ago which made the necessity to trust God much more glaring to me and everyone else around me. It is an encounter I so much want to share with you. It happened in the year 2006, on the popular Akpongbon Bridge in Lagos

Island. On that faithful night, I had just concluded a management meeting at my office in Victoria Island. I was on my way home at a few minutes past eight at night, when I ran into a terrible traffic jam. A gang of armed robbers waylaid me. They robbed me at gunpoint. No policeman was available and every other commuter focused on minding his or her business, leaving me at the mercy of the thieves. Gloria, a colleague of mine, was in a vehicle behind mine. She witnessed the incident first - hand.

To date, I still cannot answer the question everyone asked. Why did the thieves choose my car out of all the cars on the road? All I remembered was that I had just concluded a phone call when I heard an urgent tapping on the window. I was sitting in the back seat. Startled, I turned and found myself staring down the nozzle of a mean looking gun. One of the thieves was urgently tapping at the window. He instructed me to wind down the glass. I stole a quick peek at the nozzle and saw evidence of recent firing, which convinced me that the gun was a real one. I told my driver to unlock the car door, after which I opened the door by my side. Traffic was at a standstill. That ruled out all thoughts of escaping.

Shortly before then, a colleague of mine was a victim of armed robbery. It took place at his home. During the robbery, he was shot and eventually lost one of his legs. Remembering that incident, I pleaded with the thief to be merciful to me, while silently praying for God's protection. I also recalled that before thieves set out on their operations, they consume hard drugs which make them react violently to any slight provocation. This could either be because of a delay in responding to their demands or an attempt to escape from them.

I therefore listened and obeyed him. Staring ahead of me, I realized that there were several of them. While being mindful of the others, I focused on the one beside me. He snatched the phone I had just received a call with and demanded for two other phones he saw on my lap. I quickly handed them over to him. Next, he collected my purse, slung it on his shoulders, and strode off with his mates, shooting sporadically at nothing. That was when the traffic suddenly eased off and we were able to move.

Throughout the operation, I noticed that my driver was shaking with fear. After we drove off, he said that he was surprised to hear me talking to the thieves and urging them to calm down. I wondered if he expected me to argue with them.

What baffled me most was how well the thieves chose their day. Then, I used to be crazy about adorning my body with expensive gold jewelry. That day, I over indulged in this vice of mine and paid a terrible price for it. I wore a yellow gold, 18-carat Italian set of necklace and earrings. The necklace was thick, and the pendant was large. I added a bracelet, and two bold rings. In addition to these, some other valuable possessions were stolen from me. I lost fifty thousand Naira cash, checks collected from some of my clients, and my international passport. They were all inside a brown leather designer purse. While engaging the thieves, I tried to dislodge some items from my bag. I was hoping that my passport would somehow drop into the car, but I was not that lucky. The last item the thief collected from me was my purse. When he demanded for my purse, I remembered that my Divine Rosary was there. While handing it over to him, I prayed silently, prophesying; "this is your last robbery." As he walked off with members of his gang, the congested traffic started moving and we were able to continue our journey. I was infuriated when as is often the case in such circumstances, once the robbers departed, emergency sympathizers began to converge. They barraged me with very annoying questions.

Were you robbed?
Were they thieves?
What did they take from you?
Were they armed?
How many were they?

Wondering where they were when the robbery was on going, I ignored them all; slammed my car door and told my driver to move. It was a very traumatic experience for me. I knew that I needed to get out of there before I lost what was left of my sanity. I sincerely felt like I had been deprived of my precious possessions by some worthless hooligans who preferred to molest commuters on the streets of Lagos and steal from them instead of working for a living. My Passport, with which I had just processed a visa to travel abroad in two weeks, was gone. Snatched by vagabonds who had no idea what my plan was.

That night, I arrived home without a key to either my bedroom Adaora's room. My bunch of keys was in the stolen purse. The door to my bedroom was made of steel; forcing it open required a complex approach. I needed to employ the service of a welder who could only unlock my door with his welding machine, using electrical energy. That night, the notorious Nigerian Electric Power Authority (NEPA) was on break; and with them went the power supply which made it impossible for any welder to work. I found a carpenter who unlocked the door to Adaora's room, where I spent the night.

While the carpenter was still trying to unlock the door, two of my coworkers arrived. Gloria, who witnessed the robbery informed some of our colleagues within my neighborhood and they came over to my house to empathize with me. While they were busy, bemoaning my loss, I reminded them that life was much more important than possessions and advised them to join me in thanking God for sparing my life. For reasons not quite clear to me, I was confident that I could always replace whatever the thieves stole.

Much as I regretted my loss, which was at that time, a huge financial setback, I was sincerely grateful to God for saving me. I was also quite thankful for an insurance policy, which I had taken up a few months prior to the unfortunate incident. It was a householder's comprehensive policy with an all-risks extension. This meant that my mobile phones and jewelry were on a comprehensive cover and I would be paid. My coworkers who were aware of the policy kept insisting that I draw up an inventory of my loss before going to bed that night but I ignored them.

My driver repeatedly called my phones, which were still in the clutches of the thieves, pleading with them to return my International Passport. In desperation, he assured them that I did not mind parting with cash to recover my passport. Then, that was the normal practice in Lagos. When armed robbers stole your Passport, you found a way to negotiate with them. The thieves collected money from you before releasing your passport. If you were unable to pay, the thieves sold the passports to fraudulent individuals who used them to travel abroad.

That was before the emergence of the e passport system which was secured in a way that even when stolen, cannot be used by anyone but the owner. My driver was desperate on my behalf, knowing that it would be easier to recover my stolen passport than for me to go through the tedious task of processing a new one for my upcoming trip.

You Too Can Overcome Life's Challenges

As soon as my guests departed, I fell on my knees, thanking God with all my heart for sparing my life. Reminding him that I was supposed to travel abroad in fourteen days, like a child to his father, I asked why he did not make it possible for my Passport to drop off my bag and into the car during my ordeal. I then asked him how he expected me to travel without a Passport. On hindsight, I can bet God must have been laughing at me, saying "my daughter, do not worry, because you have shown gratitude, I will surprise you" but I had absolutely no idea of what was coming next.

That night, sleep eluded me. I struggled to ignore the image of the armed robber that pointed the nozzle of his gun at me. His face remained engraved in my head and all I wanted to do was banish it so that I could get some much-desired sleep. Unfortunately, that did not happen. While the rest of the world slept, I stayed up, continuously murmuring my appreciation to almighty God. I was very much aware that so many other people encountered armed robbers but were not fortunate enough to live to tell their story.

The next day, I received a call from my Managing Director, through my Driver's mobile phone. He expressed his concern over my welfare and asked me to take the day off. He was a kind and very considerate man. Relieved, I tried to relax at home, but I heard a quiet voice telling me to go to my office. When I became conscious of the message, the voice came again "Ifeoma, go to the office and collect something." I was baffled. For starters, my keys were all gone, including the key to my office drawers where I kept my cheque books. To withdraw money from the bank, I needed to request for assistance from my office and I was in no frame of mind to do so. The more I tried to ignore the instruction, the more the voice persisted until I was compelled to leave for the office. When I got downstairs and told my driver to take me to the office, he stared at me as if I was a bit unstable. When he saw me sitting inside my car, he knew that I meant what I said. Unknown to both of us, something beyond my comprehension was compelling me to go to the office.

The first person I met when I got out of the car was my Chief Finance Officer, who spent some time with me discussing my encounter with the thieves. While we were still talking, four hefty men came by, stood around us for a while, obviously listening to our conversation before going into the reception. As I walked through the reception, heading toward my office, I heard one of the men mention my name. Perplexed, I signaled to the receptionist not to reveal my identity and continued. I wondered if the thieves had succeeded in trailing me to my office. Instead of heading directly to my office, I walked into one of the offices behind the reception. I waited until Bukky; our smart receptionist joined me. She said that they were from a popular construction company. Knowing that I had no contacts in any construction company, I advised her to go back and obtain more information from the men. I ran up the stairs to my office.

I was still exchanging pleasantries with my coworkers, when Bukky burst into the room shouting;

"Madam Ifeoma! Madam Ifeoma! They said they have found your Passport"

Without a word, I jumped out of my seat and ran down the staircase to the reception with some of my colleagues in hot pursuit. None of us believed what we just heard. On our minds was a compelling question - How was it possible to recover a stolen International Passport with visas in the city of Lagos without having to negotiate with the thieves? This did not happen during the oil boom in the 1980s and 1990s. It was therefore not possible in the year 2006 when the Nigerian economy had so badly deteriorated that the ordinary man on the street was hungry and could do anything to make money.

I introduced myself to the men and requested for my Passport. They calmly explained that although one of their coworkers found it, they did not bring it with them. They explained that their colleague found my passport underneath one of the bridges where they were working. It was amongst other stolen items that the thieves discarded whilst escaping from the scene of the robbery. They said that he found some ladies purses, documents, and my Passport with my identity card beside it. He handed over the loot to their supervisor, who insisted that they should go and get me. They said that they were able to locate me by matching the identity card to the name on my Passport. Accompanied by a colleague of mine, we went to their office in Ikoyi.

Amazingly, although my passport was completely drenched, it was very much intact. Every stamp, date, and visa on it was visible and intact. Elated beyond my imagination, I danced around their office in excitement, celebrating God's accomplishment. Hugging their boss, whilst shaking hands with everyone else, tears of joy poured freely down my cheeks. This was clearly God's miracle. In his mercy, he answered my prayer and gave me back my passport. It was so perfect that it became undoubtedly glaring to me that only God could have been able to -

- Position my identity card beside my passport
- Cover the eyes of the thieves and prevent them from seeing my passport
- Make them discard my purse with its remaining contents at the construction site
- Prompt their boss to send for me as soon as she saw the recovered loot (she said that she noticed that I was a frequent traveler and felt that I may need my passport for a trip)
- Prevent the heavy rain from obliterating the data on my passport

The incident convinced me beyond any doubt of the awesomeness of God. The night the robbers struck was a very wet night. An unusual heavy rain came pouring down, drenching the loot they abandoned. My passport was spared. Nothing is beyond God. All he requires from us is a heart of gratitude. I was also very much impressed with the type of good Nigerians that found my passport, more so when they even rejected the money that I offered them for their troubles. To me, it was all the proof I needed to know that we still have some upright citizens in Nigeria. From their conduct, I became convinced that although many Nigerians are corrupt, there still exist many others that are honorable. These men were a group of Nigerians that I will always admire. God's gift to me was perfect and undoubtedly because I was grateful.

Incredibly, I dried my passport with garri – locally manufactured food from cassava tubers, and travelled two weeks later with it to the United States. I remain very grateful to God for his special mercy. Two months later, I heard that a woman was killed on the same bridge when armed robbers attacked her vehicle. They shot through the windscreen of her car, taking her life in cold blood. I heard that they were infuriated because she refused to cooperate with them. She was trying to drive off when the thieves shot at her and killed her.

In all things, it is important for you to acknowledge and give thanks to God. To him only must you give all the glory for your achievements and even your failures. When you are grateful for what he has done for you, he will do more. Life is not easy, has never been, and was not meant to be. Living a life without challenges, trials, and tribulations is not living life to the fullest. You are a child of destiny. You came to exist not by your making and had no idea that your life would turn out as it did. Your future had been pre - destined and try as you may, you can only do so much to turn things to your favor. God put you and ̄ on earth for a purpose. If you yield to his will, he will not only direct you on the path to go, but will also walk with you as you go through life. He will be with you until the very end. No matter what you are facing, he is there with you and takes you exactly to your pre-destined fate. It is important that you remember that you are never alone.

If you understand this, you will always appreciate every opportunity given to you and remain thankful to God for everything that comes your way (good or bad). All you need to do is look around you and you will realize that you have more than enough reasons to be grateful. The fact that you are alive today when so many who are younger than you are dead and gone is sufficient reason for you to be thankful.

Please, do not get it wrong. Your survival has absolutely nothing to do with how special you are or how pious you are. It is simply by the grace of God. You should therefore thank God for providing the air you breathe and the food you eat, while so many others all over the world are starving. You should thank him for the good health you enjoy, while many others are laid up in hospitals. You should also appreciate him for the gift of your children, parents, spouse, and friends. You should be grateful for your jobs, neighbors, colleagues and all the other privileges you enjoy.

It is through God's special grace and benevolence that you exist on earth. You should therefore thank him for every minute, every hour, and every second spent on earth. Remember, you have given him nothing, while he gave you everything, asking for nothing in return. Therefore, it is not too much to expect that you should love, appreciate, and honor him. When you do so, he smiles on you and showers you with more blessings.

> "AS YOU THINK ABOUT THE FUTURE .... GIVE THANKS AND TRUST GOD .... EVEN WHEN LIFE MAY BE DIFFICULT, WE SHOULD THANK GOD FOR ALL HE DOES FOR US WHICH WE DO NOT DESERVE"
> – BILLY GRAHAM

You Too Can Overcome Life's Challenges

LESSONS:

- Nothing is impossible for God
- If you want to succeed, trust God
- Prayer plus work equals success
- Miracles still happen
- Be grateful
- God's work is always perfect
- Do not argue with someone holding a gun
- In every situation give thanks to God
- Love, appreciate and trust God

CHAPTER 10

NOTHING IS IMPOSSIBLE

"WORSHIP FROM THE HEART IN TIMES OF ADVERSITY
IMPLIES AN ATTITUDE OF HUMBLE ACCEPTANCE ON OUR
PART OF GOD'S RIGHT TO DO AS HE PLEASES IN OUR
LIVES" – JERRY BRIDGES

One major lesson I learned early in life is to totally trust God, no matter the situation. Unlike what some scientists have tried to propagate, God desired that man should exist and that was why he created us. Scientists should desist from seeing human beings as existing because of an accident or some metaphysical occurrence. The bible tells us that man was pre - conceived.

He was deliberately made in the image of God and I firmly believe so. We are actually very important to our maker. To him, we are much more relevant than animals and every other thing created by God. The relevance of man was firmly stated in Mathew 6:25 – 34 – "… Look at the birds of the air: they neither sow nor reap nor gather into barns, and yet your heavenly Father feeds them. Are you not of more value than they…?" This tells us that if God feeds the swallows in the sky and the birds on the trees, how much more man, his most valuable possession, made in his own very image.

In the early 90s' I had a nasty experience when I went through a messy divorce. It was an experience I would never wish on even my worst enemy. I was in an abusive marriage. My three-year-old marriage was completely shattered and I found myself out of my matrimonial home. I was so brutally beaten up that I had to leave to save my life. It was certainly not part of my plan and I was not prepared to survive as a single woman. I married for love and it was supposed to last forever. Unfortunately, my marriage was not built to last.

You Too Can Overcome Life's Challenges

As it often happens to such mismatched marriages, it collapsed. That was after three years of struggling to make it work. We were two strangers with different values living together. Although we were a married couple, instead of building a strong union, we were working at cross-purposes. I was declaring income I made to my former husband, who felt that his duty was to make sure that it was all spent. I had no savings. I married a man who knew nothing about taking care of his responsibilities and I had to keep covering up for his lapses. I did what I believed was my duty as his wife. I spent all I earned from my job to take care of our home until we separated. I was left with a toddler to feed, clothe, and put through school. I had no help from anywhere and had to eventually turn to God. That was when I learned to trust him completely.

At first, I was very miserable. I was broken and in dire need of an encounter with God. I went through a period of depression, within which I was consuming too much alcohol. I blamed God for all my woes. I asked myself repeatedly where God was when I was being abused. I hibernated, despising myself and every other person around me. I just wanted to fly away from humanity and go to a place where I could hide. I wondered why God allowed me to go through such pain when I was sure he knew that I did not deserve it.

I was a very good example of a 'good girl' - obedient, focused, and well behaved, who met and married the man she adored. Prior to this experience, I assumed that bad things only happened to people that deserved them. I had no idea that you do not necessarily have to be evil before misfortune could befall you. I suffered so much from migraine attacks that concerned friends took me from hospitals to different pastors searching for a solution. Not only was I hopelessly young, I was also too spiritually weak to handle a failed marriage.

Something happened that roused me from a gradual plunge to permanent melancholy. While driving home from work, I almost ran into a broken-down truck parked by the side of the road. Realizing that I could have been killed, I became very scared. I thought about my life and my responsibilities. What scared me most was wondering who would take care of Adaora should my life suddenly end. I could not come up with a satisfactory answer.

That was when I realized that I had a job to do. I knew that I could not leave that responsibility for anyone else, not even her father. I had a clear idea of the standard of education and breeding I wanted Adaora to have. Although I knew that my parents would try their best, I did not want to add to their responsibilities. That was when it dawned on me that I needed to do everything possible to stay alive for her sake, and I decided to do so.

It was later that I realized that I was not totally abandoned during my travail. From the very first day, God stood by me and sent angels to assist me. I was just too troubled to recognize them. One of them was my younger sister- Chizo, whom I stayed with for a while. She stood like a rock and protected me from every attack coming from my former husband. She had to hide all the bottles of alcohol in her house to stop me from drowning my sorrows in them.

Pearl was another angel, God sent her to me when I attended a training program for bank executives. That was few weeks before the collapse of my marriage. I met Pearl on the very first day of the training. Our eyes met when I walked into the room. She beckoned on me and offered me the seat by her side. We got on so well that we sat next to each other throughout the three-day program. That was how our friendship started. Pearl later turned out to be very supportive to me when I found myself out of my matrimonial home. She accommodated me in her apartment for a while, despite facing persecution for doing so. We spent time praying together and I was deeply encouraged by her passion for our Lord Jesus Christ.

She was a former member of the old Scripture Union and a serious 'born again' Christian. Recently, I saw her again after several years and was not surprised to learn that she has become a Deaconess. A position I would gladly recommend for anyone like her who selflessly cares so much for people going through hardship. Over the years, I watched her sacrifice so much for others that it sometimes weighed her down. Although married and running a family of her own, I am sure she remains as caring as she was when we first met.

There was also Uche, my friend and colleague who stood by me like a guardian angel. My daughter, Adaora was first to call her an angel. Through my separation and divorce, Uche was always there for me. She tirelessly helped me through the most difficult moments of my life, even when she felt I did not appreciate her enough. Her older sister Nkechi supported me financially and spent lots of her valuable time advising and encouraging me.

They still do not have any idea how much I appreciate them because most times words cannot adequately express the overwhelming gratitude our hearts feel. We bonded like sisters from the same parents and I knew that I could always trust them. I also remember Tonia, who was married to my ex- husband's cousin. She took me to several Pastors while we searched for ways of mending my broken marriage. Tonia has been serving as a Pastor in South Africa for years.

Rebecca was another angel. She was my longtime friend and colleague. We met at the Government media house where I worked. At first, Rebecca could not understand what went wrong with my seemingly perfect marriage. She however, stood by me and defended me while others were judging me. Unfortunately, she did not know that her marriage was also crumbling, until it ended. She remains one of my true friends. The painful divorce we both experienced bonded us together. Like me, Rebecca also had to train her daughter as a single parent.

Another set of angels are Dr. George Okwerekwu and his beautiful wife Dr. Irene Okwerekwu who are Medical Doctors. Although they are relations of my former husband, they stood by me and gave me every support I needed to go on with my life. They were the sponsors at our wedding and therefore in the best position to know the true story of our collapsed marriage. In every step of the way towards my survival, God used them to relieve my sorrows.

I drew strength from all my angels in different ways but had no idea that they were there to rescue me from drowning. I became even stronger when I came across a write up on 'The Wilderness Experience.' It was in a publication of 'Every Day with Jesus.' This religious booklet explained that when we go through crisis, it is not because God has abandoned us. Instead, God allows us to experience certain misfortunes in life to make us stronger human beings. Just as raw gold is burnt in fire to refine it, he puts us through pain to increase our faith in him and prepares us better for the roles we are to play while on our earthly sojourn.

The publication went on to clarify that it is not that God has forgotten us, but that he stays by our side even at the time of our trials and sees us through. That explains why we survive while some other people who have gone through similar trials do not. It went further to explain that when the trial is over, we emerge much stronger than we were before it began. This publication became a major eye - opener for me. I bought two additional copies, which I mailed to my parents with a letter. There, I explained my new understanding of the unfortunate situation in which I found myself and emphasized my unwavering determination to survive. Then I turned to God in prayer, saying the following words;

"Lord Jesus, now I know that you have been with me since the beginning and you are still with me. You are aware of my situation and you know that I have a little child to nurture. Father, we are in this together, you and I, and you must see me through"

From that day, I began to trust God completely and call on him any time I needed help. I told him how much money I had left in my wallet. I voiced out what I precisely needed for myself, for my daughter's education and upkeep and for my dependents. I made him realize that I relied totally on him for sustenance. I can confirm to you that he was very faithful.

From that day, onwards, he adequately provided for us. He walked with me and warned me of any intending danger. He showed me events that were going to happen, long before they occurred. Most times, the visions came during the daytime, not even in my dreams. Sometimes, they were quite scary. I began to live a more purposeful life. Although I had several other trials, and spiritual attacks, I am convinced without any iota of doubt that it was by trusting God that I was able to overcome all of them. When I talk to the younger ones that I mentor; I stand tall to tell to them that I am a living miracle and a testimony that miracles still happen. The fact that I am still alive is also a miracle. I will share some of my miracles with you, hoping that that you too can learn to trust God and enjoy all the blessings that come from relying totally on him.

One beautiful morning, in the year 1997, I woke up with a swollen left eye. It was protruding so much that I had to check in to see an ophthalmologist. The doctor suspected that it was thyroid deficiency that led to the swelling. I went to several private hospitals, hoping that one of the doctors could come up with a more acceptable diagnosis. Eventually, I was placed on hormonal drugs. My eyes were bulging so much that anyone that knew me could instantly recognize that something had seriously gone wrong with my eyes.

You Too Can Overcome Life's Challenges

I ran into Tina, a longtime friend of mine on Opebi Road. We had not seen for several years because she was living in the United Kingdom. Tina's reaction was very passionate. She came very close to tears as she demanded to know what happened to me. I calmly explained that I was receiving treatment for thyroid deficiency. We prayed together and she went away promising to check on me from time to time. I continued with the prescription.

While getting dressed on a Sunday morning, I felt a dizzy sensation but did not want to miss going to church. My car was at the mechanic workshop. I and Adaora went by public transport. Although I was weak, I was so determined to make it to church that nothing could have stopped me. We were walking to the bus station when I collapsed by the roadside. I was holding Adaora's hand before this happened. Other pedestrians came to my rescue and revived me. They found a chair in front of a house for me to rest for a while before continuing the journey home. I was thoroughly embarrassed.

Weeks later, my health deteriorated. I needed to find out what was wrong with my eye, so I kept searching. I consulted another Ophthalmologist in one of the government hospitals who sent me to their laboratory for some tests. It was consoling to know that someone was keen on finding out exactly what was wrong with me instead of guessing. Since I had been going to the other hospitals, no test was ever done. It was when I went to collect the test result that the Holy Spirit spoke to me through the Lab Technician. As he handed over the lab result to me, he uttered the following words;

'My sister, go and pray. There is nothing wrong with you. It is spiritual"

I looked at the lab result and saw that it was negative.

I was astonished because I had earlier suspected that the three doctors, I earlier consulted were wrong when they diagnosed thyroid deficiency. One of them went to the extent of recommending that surgery was required to correct the physical distortion of my eyes. It was such a relief to know that they were all wrong. Broken and completely helpless, I concluded that it was only God that could heal me. When I got home that evening, I stared at my mirror in tears for a very long time. Wiping away my tears, I called on my God to help me. It was a simple prayer, said straight from a very distressed heart.

Father Lord, you have seen my eyes. I do not know what is wrong with me and have no idea how it came about. I have offended no one and cannot afford to lose my eyes. I also do not have money to pay for any eye surgery. Lord Jesus, please restore my eyes. I need my eyes back. It was like a prayer said by a little child, asking his father for help.

That night, I cried until I slept off. In the morning, I looked at the mirror, and was stunned to see that my eyes were back to normal. Apparently, I received my healing while still sleeping. It was as if God had given me a new set of eyes. They were so bright and beautiful that it was as if nothing was ever wrong with them. I began to jump up and down with joy. Next, I fell on my knees, thanking God for his mercy. When Adaora woke up and realized what happened, she confirmed that my eyes were fully restored. It was undoubtedly a miracle.

Tina became aware of the miracle when she came to visit me before returning to the UK. She was thrilled to discover that I had been healed. I wasted no time in sharing my testimony with her. She joined me in thanking and praising God for the gift of his miracle. I still remember her exact words;

Ify, it is God o! Thank God for your life. It is only God that could have done this for you.

And my response was – Who else, my dear. Who else but God?

So many other miracles followed. There was a gas explosion in my kitchen that left me totally unhurt. I had just serviced my gas cocker before travelling to Port Harcourt, the capital city of Rivers state. After a prolonged delay at the airport, I arrived home very hungry. I decided to quickly make some chicken noodle soup. Just as I lit the gas burner, I heard a loud noise that vibrated past me. It was a whoosh kind of sound. The escaping gas tore the net attached to my kitchen door frame and escaped, into the open air. Trembling, but still on my feet, I quickly switched off the gas cooker and ran through my dining area into the living room where I examined my body. To my greatest delight, except for some tingling on parts of my skin, I was fully intact. I called my friend that I left behind in Port Harcourt and broke the news of my latest miracle. We celebrated it together with more thanks to God.

Another miracle was an electrical fire outbreak in my bedroom. The fire emanated from the cable of a standing fan. I was asleep with

You Too Can Overcome Life's Challenges

Adaora right beside me when it happened. That night as in many other nights, she refused to sleep in her room. Somehow in the wee hours of the morning, I suddenly stirred. I was shocked to see a burning flame in the middle of my room. Still very drowsy, I dragged myself out of the bed, muttering "Jesus."

Then, I stood before the fire and blew it out with one breath. I know it sounds bizarre, but that was exactly what happened. Up until date, I still cannot explain how it was possible. It was all like a dream. I believe that I may have been in a trance since I could not remember rationalizing what I was doing, but I assure you that it did happen. I must have slept off again until the following morning. It was a Sunday morning. I remember jumping out of bed the moment I recalled the fire. I ran to confirm that it really happened. That was when I saw the scorched patch of my rug.

Surprisingly, it was only a little piece of my rug that was affected. As if to further confirm the incident, the burnt piece of cord from the standing fan lay lifeless on the rug. That was when it dawned on me that it was a fire outbreak. Adaora and I, just escaped being burnt to death. Unaware of the fire incident, Adaora continued sleeping until I woke her up and showed her the burnt rug. We held hands and danced around the room in celebration, while praising God. After prayers that morning, she suddenly turned and calmly said to me "Mummy, it was the Holy Spirit that woke you up and asked you to blow out the burning flame." I was so touched with her insight and responded, "Yes my darling, it was." I marveled at her conviction at the tender age of eight.

My next miracle was a pot of water that survived through the night sitting on my ignited gas burner. Although the water was all dried up, the pot was still sitting on the gas burner with a powder - like white substance in it until the following morning. The water was meant for my bath, but I must have been too tired that I dozed off and did not stir until the following morning. I turned off the gas, wondering why the shape of the pot was not distorted and how the fire was contained.

While still trusting God and believing totally in him, he continued to bless me with other encounters of answered prayers. I will share one more remarkable miracle with you that became the turning point in my life. This was an incident that sealed my faith in the absolute power of God to enable us accomplish what hitherto seemed impossible. It was also a firm confirmation to me that everything God predestined will surely come to pass and nothing or no one has the power to stop them from happening. I am also convinced that if you trust and believe in him, you too can and will experience great miracles. God truly loves us and he continues to bless us with his miracles. It is up to us to recognize and acknowledge the miracles we receive. As the years unfolded, it turned out that he had more in stock for me.

God blessed me with a beautiful daughter, who at the age of eight decided that she wanted to be a medical doctor. She was good in both arts and sciences and could have gone for any other discipline, but chose medicine. My father taught me that a parent should never compel his child to study any course to satisfy his personal desire. Her late father was pushing for her to go for engineering. I advised him that it was better for her to choose her professional course. instead of making choices for her. This is because if a child chooses what he wants to study, he will be better disposed to accepting responsibility, should he encounter any challenge while in school, knowing that he made that choice. It is like choosing a life partner for a man or woman. If you do so, be sure to get the blame for whatever goes wrong in the marriage even if the same person does not appreciate you when things go well.

Adaora's choice did not actually come as a surprise because there are many doctors and nurses in our family. Being a single parent, I wondered how I could cope with the enormous fees and prolonged years of study. Something happened that convinced me that it was her destiny to study medicine. It was the day we had an encounter with a mentally deranged man at Allen Roundabout in Ikeja.

I was walking towards Allen Avenue from Aromire Street. I had my hand firmly clasped on top of Adaora's hand when I saw a roughly dressed and dirty looking man approaching us. His feet were bare and on his frame was strung decorative amulets. He was coming from the opposite direction. When he suddenly crossed over to where we were, we moved aside to make space for him; he smiled at me and muttered "Iya doctor", and walked by.

Startled, I asked Adaora if she heard what the man said. She gave me a beautiful smile, saying, but I told you so. "Iya doctor" means mother of a doctor in Yoruba language. It was like a message from heaven and an authentication of her calling but I had no clue how it would come to pass. Over the years, it had been a struggle to meet up with settling our bills. House rent, feeding and school fees were already a huge struggle. I had no clue how I was supposed to cope with sponsoring a medical doctor. My salary was not sufficient to train a medical doctor. That was in the year 1997 and Adaora was only eight years old.

In 2006, Adaora gained admission to study Biological Sciences at the University of Ghana. This was a prelude for entering their prestigious Medical School. I managed to pay her fees and sent her off to school. A year later, she took the examination to the medical school and passed both the written and oral test, but was not granted admission. According to the school authorities, there was limited allocation for foreign students. She was clearly devastated, especially since her father had just recently passed on. Fulfilling her dream would have cheered her up.

Three of her friends whom we all held hands to pray before they went for the oral interview were successful. Adaora's GPA was better than that of some of them, leaving her feeling very disappointed and deeply hurt. Watching my daughter cry with disappointment made my heart bleed.

I decided to go to the school to find out what could have happened. There, I met some of the administrative staff who could not give me any cogent reason why her name was not on the admission list. I tried to see the Dean of their College of Medicine but she refused to meet with any parent. The Chief Executive Officer (CEO) of the Advertising Company where I worked who was a Ghanaian tried to see the Dean of the Faculty of Medicine on my behalf but could not. We were later informed that there was too much pressure from parents of foreign students whose children could not gain admission that she chose to avoid us all.

We were also informed that some Nigerian senators came with bags of money to bribe their way through to get their children into the medical school. Ghana had been very careful to maintain a high academic standard in their universities. Being an indigene, my boss accompanied me because he believed in my daughter and thought his presence could make a difference. We made more effort to see the Dean, but it was all in vain. While we persisted, one of the administrative staff of the college questioned Adaora's conviction in wanting to study medicine. He cited her age as a good reason why he thought she should first graduate from Biological Sciences. He said that she needed to be matured enough to be definite about what she wanted to study, before seeking admission to their medical school.

At that time, Adaora was only seventeen. He said he believed that she was too young. He did not understand how she could be so convinced at such a young age, but I did. I am her mother. I knew how determined she was to become a medical doctor. I trusted Adaora and was sure that she knew exactly what she wanted. She even became more determined after her father died from battling brain cancer for years. While trying to explain my daughter's desire to be a doctor, I cried with disappointment at the hopeless picture he painted for me. He told me that all the spots were filled. There was a limited allocation for foreign students and it was all taken.

While I continued crying at the thought of my precious daughter missing out on such a wonderful opportunity, he painted a picture of hopelessness for me. It was not my plan to cry in front of anyone about the situation. I had always considered myself to be a strong woman who did not cry easily over anything, but I was in a desperate situation and had been stretched to my limit. Before I left his office; I promised him that I was not prepared to give up on Adaora's admission. He was looking at me with a lot of pity, and doubt. The look of despondency on his face made me wipe away my tears in defiance. Rising from my chair, I stood proudly in front of him and pronounced

"Sir, I will not give up. If it is God's will, my daughter will still be offered an admission to study medicine in this school."

I walked out of his office.

I followed up with so many other unsuccessful visits to the school. I met many other hopeful candidates and their parents. Some of the students were so desperate that they started attending lectures in the College of Medicine, while hoping to be enrolled. Although some of her friends were asking her to join them in the medical school, I did not think it was appropriate for someone who was yet to be offered an admission to start attending classes. I advised Adaora not to confuse herself by joining them. Some people believe that the best way to solve a problem is by relying on human strength or by physical resistance. Being tactical is beyond the physical.

Instead of physically resisting the situation, we decided to go on our knees. I called my mother and siblings and requested for prayers.

You Too Can Overcome Life's Challenges

It became a family battle. My daughter was exceptionally brilliant. Every member of my family was very much aware that medicine was her choice of profession and therefore saw the situation as very critical. They also knew that she became more determined after her father died from a brain tumor. He died after enduring two unsuccessful surgeries. We were certain that her life would never be the same if she failed to fulfill her dream. Every member of my family offered fervent prayers towards Adaora's admission to medical school. Without discussing with her, I made a secret vow to God. Realizing how hopeless the situation was, Adaora also made a personal vow without knowing that I had done the same.

At this time, my mother was living in the United States. She was a very prayerful woman and frequently visited the Blessed Sacrament at the altar as true Catholics usually do.

On one of her frequent visits to the Blessed Sacrament, she received a message that Adaora should pick up the Prayer Rosary and pray it every day. She called and informed me. I got her a new Rosary made sure it was blessed by a priest and told her to start praying with it, just as my mother said. She went back to school, registered for second year in the faculty of Biological Sciences and continued with her classes.

One month later, I was wrapped up with work in my office when my phone beeped. It was a text message from the Registrar in the College of Medicine. The text read-

It is a yes! Bring your daughter for registration, immediately.

I jumped out of my seat shouting -

"Jesus! Oh my God! Thank you, Jesus!"

I ran to my chairman's office to inform him. Stunned, he stared at me, speechless for a while, then finding his voice, he asked, and what are you still doing here?

Laughing with joy, I sprang out of his office.

He knew how important it was for my daughter to get into Medical School. Having accompanied me to the school a couple of times to see the Dean, he also understood how impossible it seemed until that day. He therefore recognized that a miracle had just happened. The heavens opened and God answered our prayers. It was amazing. I felt like jumping around and announcing the delightful news to everyone. That was the moment I remembered that I had not informed Adaora.

I picked up my phone and called her. For a while, she was silent. I guess she was processing what she just heard.

Nne, are you still there? I asked.

In a very tiny voice, she responded.

Mummy, I am here. I do not even know what to say.

You do not have to say anything.

Where are you? I asked.

I am in the Lab, she replied

Just take off your lab coat and be on standby. I am coming to pick you up so that we can go and collect your admission letter.

I neither got a response nor waited for one.

From the lab we went straight to the Registrar's office where we collected her admission letter. We detected an error in her name and insisted on waiting until it was amended before leaving the school. I did not want to take any chances. While we were waiting, the Administrative Officer in whose office I wept requested to see me. This was the same man who was not convinced that Adaora was matured enough to study medicine because of her age. When he saw me, he confessed in the following words – Madam, your faith has seen you through

He reminded me of the statement I made before leaving his office during my last visit – that I will not give up and that if it is God's will, their school will still offer admission to my daughter. I smiled, remembering how desperate I was.

Adaora was completely speechless. She was in a state of stupor. I realized that her body was burning up with fever and decided to take her home. Although I was a bit worried about her extreme reaction to the great news, I knew that it was because she had almost given up. Who in her position would not give up, when her mates in the medical school had been attending lectures for over a month?

She found it so difficult to believe that she had received the miracle we were praying for and was going to fulfill her dream of becoming a medical doctor. It was later that night, when her friends and classmates started calling to congratulate her that she realized that it was true, then she whispered to me -

Mummy, so I am going to study medicine.

Yes, my darling, I responded.

You Too Can Overcome Life's Challenges

Later, I heard that five students were shortlisted for one supplementary slot. That was because one of the successful Ghanaian candidates did not show up. The Dean chose Adaora because she scored the highest mark in the written test. This explanation was not adequate for me because should that have been the case, why was her name not on the initial list? The fact that the Dean whom we never met was the same person that eventually selected her left me marveling at the way God works. He performs his miracles in ways that we can never really understand.

All that transpired so far showed that it was the hand of God straightening the way for my dear daughter and that was because we placed our trust in him. God always performs miracles for us so that his name will be glorified. We only need to trust him.

Most times when I look at Adaora who has been a Medical Doctor since 2013, I remember how merciful God has been to us. I have been truly humbled and remain in absolute awe of how reliable and faithful God really is. Adaora has grown to be a strong and determined young woman. She learned so much from watching me go through loads of challenges and eventually succeed. Although she too had experienced other trials, even as a child, there is no doubt that this further strengthened her faith in God. I am definite that her struggles better prepared her for the service she has been delivering in the field of psychiatry in the United Kingdom.

Earlier, she failed to secure admission into a Federal Government college despite an excellent score in the Common Entrance Examination. Her invitation letter for the verbal interview went missing while in transit. She had to be enrolled into a private secondary school in Lagos. Subsequently, she gained admission to study in the United States but was not granted a Visa despite her tuition fee having been fully paid. She missed out on a golden opportunity but God had other plans. For a struggling, single parent, it was a huge impediment for me because her admission offer came with a fifty percent scholarship. Up until date, I still remember how she wept as we left the American embassy in Nigeria. She felt humiliated and rejected. I was very bitter, knowing that she was hurt but consoled her as best as I could. I told her not to worry, that it was probably not God's plan for her to study in the United States. Years later, when she returned from visiting the

United States, United Kingdom, and Switzerland, she kept staring at her Passport. When I asked why, she said;

Mummy, I cannot believe that this is my passport with so many Visas.

I shook my head and smiled, glorifying God for his grace upon our lives. You must learn to align with God's plans for your life, else you can make a lot of effort and achieve nothing. When your plans are in harmony with God's plans, you achieve a lot more with less effort.

Adaora's first trip to the UK was in the year 2010. Since then, a lot has happened. For someone both the United States and UK embassies denied Visa several times, she could not but marvel at how things turned around. I am quite confident that she would spend the rest of her life like a true Christian woman, absolutely believing and trusting God. In life, there will always be hurdles, but you must learn to go through them with faith. If you trust God, nothing is impossible. When God says it is time, even the impossible becomes possible.

LESSONS:

- Although trials will always come, God never abandons us
- When we are in need, God sends angels to help us
- God allows us to experience certain misfortunes in life to make us stronger people
- When in distress, talk to God, he never fails
- When praying and asking God for a favor, be specific
- Acknowledge the miracles in your life and appreciate God
- Never give up because nothing is impossible for God
- Always let your faith speak for you
- When God says it is time, even the impossible becomes possible

CHAPTER 11

BE PATIENT

"HE THAT CAN HAVE PATIENCE CAN HAVE WHAT HE WILL"
– BENJAMIN FRANKLIN

To be successful in any relationship, a lot of patience is required. Patience brings peace. Impatient people are often unable to handle challenges. Patience makes it possible for you to see clearly and make rational decisions. A relationship often starts with excitement because an adventure is just beginning. There is an air of expectation and eagerness on both parties to explore. As the relationship progresses and partners get to know more about each other, they discover character traits and behavioral patterns hitherto undisclosed. This may lead to a certain level of discomfort or irritation. If there is no immediate effort to work on such thorny areas, the euphoria fizzles out and the relationship becomes boring and may even collapse. At this stage in every relationship, patience and tolerance play major roles.

Patience is truly a virtue and a garment that anyone who wants to succeed must wear. To achieve your dreams, you should stay focused, while patiently and deliberately pursuing them. Even if you fail, do not give up on your dreams. Instead, spend time to review your strategies, make the necessary changes and keep trying. When you are criticized, be patient with the person criticizing you. He is probably just an agent, being used to propel you to greater heights. Pay attention to the criticisms, you probably will learn something from them that will make you a better person. Do not ever give up on your dreams. Trust God and pray fervently, even as you continue to work towards achieving them. God never fails.

With patience, a couple can deal effectively with their challenges. This would make their relationship become stronger. Patience helps partners understand each other better.

My father came out of his bedroom and walked straight into my mother's room, shouting (more like yelling her name);

"Maggiee! Maggiee!"

Not the Maggie of Maggie cubes, a favorite Nigerian spice. This was his affectionate way of shortening my mother's name - Magdalene.

She jumped out of bed, anxious to find out what crime she had committed. They met at the door to her room.

Where are those pictures, I gave you? He asked. What pictures? My mother innocently responded.

That got him snapping in a harsh tone -

Those pictures we took at the wedding we attended yesterday.

She tried again to come up with the right answer -

You did not give them to me; you took them to your room.

Wrong answer again - we could tell by the contortion of my father's face that he was even more furious with her. Ignoring her protest; he adamantly insisted that she must produce the pictures before walking off in a huff. In exasperation, she turned to us, her willing spectators in this re-occurring drama of love.

Ewo! Your father has started again, she exclaimed in exasperation.

I and my sisters knew what was coming next and quickly moved towards her to console her. She pleaded with us to come and help her find the pictures. As we searched and turned over every cushion and mattress in all the rooms and halls in our home, she kept on appealing to us to find the pictures and save her from my father's wrath.

She said that she was aware that no matter how hard she tried to convince him; my father would never accept that he did not give the pictures to her. After three hours of rigorously combing the whole house, we found the pictures on top of a bedside stool in my father's room. There were some documents placed on them. What surprised me most was my mother's reaction -

Thank God. Now we can have some peace in this house. Your father will never stop blaming me for everything that goes wrong.

She sighed and continued with her chores.

For me, that was tolerance in its best form. My mother had the kind of patience that made it possible for her marriage to my father to have lasted forever. Not surprising anyone that knew them, my parents lived peacefully together as husband and wife for over fifty years until my father died from prostate cancer.

You Too Can Overcome Life's Challenges

Let us examine this scenario from a different perspective. Assuming my mother's reaction had been different, tempers would have risen, and she may have said something she would later regret. She may have been too angry to find the pictures, and my parents would have spent some valuable time nursing bitterness for each other. Tolerance stems from maturity. If we acknowledge that God has made us different and with divergent behavioral patterns, then we should learn to tolerate one another's excesses, failures, and mistakes.

I took a keen interest in my mother's reaction to my father's missing items and realized that it was because she understood that he was not just trying to make her miserable. The fact was that over time, he had formed the habit of entrusting to her, valuable items that he wanted to be kept safe. He knew that whenever he needed them, she would produce them. On the other hand, being quite an intelligent woman, my mother was able to recollect every item that was in her custody. She could also remember which items were not given to her. This was a rare talent she had which my father refused to appreciate. However, instead of making it an issue, she remained tolerant, knowing that his ultimate motive was to find what was missing. She was convinced that he loved her and therefore could not have wanted to make her miserable by ridiculing her.

Intolerance arises from misconception, lack of trust, perception, and misunderstanding of motives. Broad-minded people are often more tolerant than others. Nothing leads to impatience more than ignorance and lack of experience. It is always better when people learn to relieve their minds of stored up baggage by expressing themselves (speaking out). Then, and only then can they begin to trust again.

If someone has been restricted to certain ways of life, religion, and culture without having experienced any other, he may believe that what he knows is the very best. Often, this leads to his being less tolerant of other people's language, religion, and culture, which he does not understand and has never experienced. This may help us begin to appreciate why there has been so much rancor, lack of understanding, religious and cultural disagreements between indigenes of different tribes and countries.

We should be grateful for the technological advancement and opportunities available in recent times that make it possible for someone to easily fly from one country to another, and enjoy firsthand, cuisines and cultural practices of other people. It is now possible for someone to sit in the comfort of their home and take a visual trip via the internet to appreciate beautiful cultures that are much unlike what exists in their immediate environment. Understanding other people's way of life makes us more tolerant of their belief systems.

Tolerance is vital for the success of any relationship. Being able to appreciate that man has been specially crafted and equipped with diverse talents, everyone being different from the other and having something peculiar to offer, should make us more tolerant towards one another. Coming to terms with the fact that no one is perfect and that everyone has flaws; recognizing that there is good and bad in every human being, is a first step to learning how to appreciate the goodness in others. Acknowledging that everyone has positive and negative attributes will help us tolerate each other's flaws and enable us to build longer lasting relationships.

A beautiful relationship can only exist when both parties learn how to respect and appreciate each other's attributes, while playing down their character flaws. Character flaws always affect relationships. It is only when someone is not close to you, that you can assume that he is perfect. Once there is a relationship between two people, their positive and negative traits become obvious. When selfish interests sometimes overcome their collective interest, their flaws begin to show.

When a husband and wife truly begin to see each other as their better half or missing rib, they may start finding and harnessing what they lack from their partner. The sooner a partner recognizes that his spouse is a blessing and was designed to make up for his lapses; he begins to see her as a necessary spare part to his incomplete engine. Soon after, he realizes that just like a car's engine, she needs to be oiled and serviced regularly for ultimate performance.

To be candid, everyone is occasionally uptight, behaves irrationally, and exhibits some elements of madness. The ability of the next person to go beyond reacting to the moment of madness in the drama of life and instead place himself in the other person's position, the more prepared he is to accommodate the irrational behavior. It is only when he can do so that he can truly forgive and tolerate that person. That is the true meaning of maturity.

Being able to tolerate what you cannot change and adapt to any given situation helps a great deal in achieving true happiness. What has helped me in my journey to maturity is my ability to recite and abide by the serenity prayer by Reinhold Niebuhr. Perhaps, if everyone learns how to recite and truly practice the words of this prayer, they will be in a better position to live a life of tranquility -

THE SERENITY PRAYER
"GOD, GRANT ME THE SERENITY TO ACCEPT THE THINGS I
CANNOT CHANGE; COURAGE TO CHANGE THE THINGS I CAN;
AND WISDOM TO KNOW THE DIFFERENCE. LIVING ONE DAY AT
A TIME ..."

REINHOLD NEIBUHR

This is exactly how life was meant to be lived – one day at a time, bearing no grudge and therefore walking baggage free.

> "ALL HUMAN WISDOM IS SUMMED UP IN TWO WORDS – WAIT AND HOPE"
> – ALEXANDER DUMAS PE'RE

LESSONS:

- Patience brings peace
- Even if you fail, do not give up on your dreams
- Patience helps partners understand each other
- Someone criticizing you is just an agent propelling you to greater heights
- God never fails
- No one is perfect
- Learn to accept what you cannot change
- When praying and asking God for a favor, be specific
- Recognize the miracles in your life and appreciate God
- Broadminded people are often more tolerant than others
- Ignorance and lack of exposure leads to impatience
- Impatient people are often unable to handle challenges
- Patience is a garment that anyone that wants to succeed must wear
- See your spouse as a necessary spare part to your incomplete engine
- Everyone is occasionally uptight, behaves irrationally and exhibits elements of madness

CHAPTER 12

SAVE AND INVEST FOR TOMORROW

> **"I USED TO SAY WHY SAVE MONEY IF I'LL DIE TOMORROW, I HAVEN'T DIED YET AND I HAVE NOTHING TO SURVIVE ON"**
> **– BANGAMBIKI HABYARIMANA**

No matter what your income may be, put something aside for tomorrow. I am a firm believer in the idiom "saving for a rainy day". Some people erroneously believe that until they are earning big, they cannot save. The truth is that if you cannot save when your income is low, you will find it difficult to do so when your income increases. It really does not matter how much you earn. You must learn to always put something aside.

When I was a child, I began saving by putting aside a fraction of my pocket money in a little tin. It was called 'kom – kom' in our local dialect. It served as our piggy bank. Although what I saved up did not amount to anything substantial, it was very useful, especially when I ran out of pocket money and could not convince my parents to find some extra cash for me. I had the kind of parents that believed that overindulging a child will ruin him while denying him sometimes helps to make him stronger. That was how I learned how to save.

In college, while some of my friends finished their allowance within the first two weeks of resumption, I structured mine in such a way that it lasted until my next allowance was due. Knowing that students were resuming, some traders came with their goods to hawk within the campus. Clothes, shoes, and bags were often on display in the female hostels. Without discipline, it was almost impossible to resist spending all your money on frivolities.

As soon as I started working, 'kom – kom' transformed to a savings account where I made sure I always set aside a percentage of my income that I could fall back on. Eventually, I began to invest in shares of viable companies. I did not stop there. While still struggling with paying Adaora's school fees, I continued to look out for other opportunities where I could utilize any reasonable extra fund in my possession. I found out that what I was able to save kept me going even in the most difficult times.

From experience, I would always recommend investing in real estate. I tried partnership, but it did not work for me. All investments I made towards growing other people's businesses failed and the people I tried working with always had sad stories to tell. I learned my lessons, cut my losses, and moved on, vowing not to ever go into any form of partnership. I did not stop investing because I recognize that it is always better to dare than to sit back and imagine how bleak or successful the result would have been. Saving makes you confident and prepares you for the unexpected.

Every parent should do their children a huge favor of teaching them how to save. This is because their investments and savings are what will give them succor when they are old. That is when they will no longer be energetic and able to jump out of bed in the early hours of the morning to rush to work. It may also be difficult for them to endure the hustle and bustle of working, to earn monthly income. At that time whatever funds they were able to save will become very useful.

> "FINANCIAL PEACE ISN'T THE ACQUISITION OF STUFF. IT IS THE LEARNING TO LIVE ON LESS THAN YOU MAKE, SO YOU CAN GIVE MONEY BACK AND HAVE MONEY TO INVEST. YOU CAN'T WIN UNTIL YOU DO THIS"
> – DAVE RAMSEY

LESSONS:

- If you cannot save when your income is low, you will find it difficult to save when it increases
- Parents should teach their children how to save
- Save while you are still strong
- Saving requires discipline

CHAPTER 13

PLAN YOUR LIFE

> "YOU WERE BORN TO WIN, BUT TO BE A WINNER, YOU MUST PLAN TO WIN, PREPARE TO WIN, AND EXPECT TO WIN."
> – ZIG ZIGLAR

Plan to succeed, with faith. Imagine going through life without a plan. What kind of life would that be? Anyone who goes through day to day living without a plan can best be described as a man that has no vision. He has no dreams and therefore makes no plans to achieve them. When you plan, you have a direction. Planning does not only help you to focus but ensures that you do not fail. Your plan is your driving force. The human mind is very strong. If you can think it, you can achieve it.

Since it is up to you to determine whether you want to succeed or not, it is also up to you to think about succeeding and therefore plan to achieve success. Planning is all about making decisions that help you to control your life. If you really want to avoid embarrassing situations in your life, you must start planning. Otherwise, you may be caught unawares by unpaid bills and unforeseen situations. Planning helps you prepare for the unexpected.

The moment I started working, while still doing my National Youth Service, I stopped accepting money from my parents. It was a decision I was compelled to make because I knew that there were five younger siblings of mine that were still in school. The first time I visited our home in Enugu from my location in Calabar, my mother attempted to pay for my return ticket. She was surprised when I rejected her offer. She persisted, until I explained to her that I planned the trip and came home with enough transport fare for my journey back to Calabar. I will never forget the look of admiration on her face and how she said;

"If you need any help, please let me know."

You Too Can Overcome Life's Challenges

I knew that the statement was well intended because she was always willing to part with anything she had, if any of her children ever needed it. Unknown to her, she had just given me the encouragement I needed to work even harder in my determination to cater for myself. I knew that my parents had done so well to have paid my school fees from primary school up to the university level. Full of appreciation for the gift of sound education they gave me, I vowed to do my very best to make them proud of their accomplishment. The best way to achieve my dreams was by being proactive and very productive. That way, I could remain relevant enough to cover milestones of achievements. I had to choose where best to begin my career and sought to join a media house.

There was an embargo on employment and I had no one to assist me. Propelled by my dream, plan, and faith in God, I convinced my elder sister to accompany me to our national television station. I had already chosen the exact department I wanted to work in and therefore went straight to the Director of News. Fortunately, we were able to gain entrance to his office which was not an easy achievement. He was a very imposing man and I was very young. I remember how he looked at us from the top of his glasses and with a deep voice asked what he could do for us. Somewhere from within me, a voice spoke;

"I need a job, sir and I would like to work with you, as a News Reporter. I could tell that he was shocked at my audacity but was kind enough not to show it. He smiled, asked us to sit down and immediately put me through my first interview. If he meant to discourage me, he failed. I answered all his questions like someone that was expecting an interview. The questions were typical interview questions;

Where did you graduate from?

What class of degree did you make?

What makes you think you can work here?

Why do you want to be a journalist?

What are your strengths and weaknesses?

What do you have to offer?

He made it clear to me that being a journalist was not child's play and I assured him that I was ready for a tough job. He was obviously so impressed with my responses that he apologized because the Nigerian government had placed an embargo on the employment of Government workers. He promised that as soon as it became possible, he would place me on their interview list. That was all I needed. I thanked him and went home to pray, while following up with frequent trips to his office. I waited for months, nothing happened but I never gave up.

Although I was occupying my uncle's Boys' quarters on Adeola Odeku Street, Victoria Island, I had no job and therefore no salary. I survived by writing drama scripts for the programs department of the same Television house and modelling for an advertising agency. My parents summoned me back to Enugu to pick up a teaching job. I refused to leave Lagos and continued to push for the job I wanted. It was a highly competitive job and very difficult to get. No one else saw any possibility of my eventually working in that television house, except me. When it was time, God made it possible using the same Director of News.

It happened on the day I almost gave up. My bags were packed and I was ready to take the next available bus back to Enugu. My parents called and threatened to disown me if I remained in Lagos. Someone fed them stories about how young girls were parading themselves on the streets of Lagos, becoming victims of irresponsible men who were scouting for free women to satisfy their lust. They were told that I was being deceived and had perhaps become one of the numerous mistresses of such men. They did not understand how I was able to survive living in Lagos without what they considered a real job. There was no one to defend me. My resources were depleting.

One of my drama scripts had been stolen and used by someone else to enrich himself. I was shocked to watch the story I wrote shown on television with credit awarded to someone else. I had no idea how that could have happened and was in no position to contest it. I cried throughout the night. The next morning, I decided to make a final attempt by going to the television house that morning before leaving Lagos. The Director of News was in a board meeting. I went over to the boardroom where a security man stopped me from entering. I introduced myself and told him that I was there to see the director and that it was very important. Instead of turning me away, he gave me a piece of paper to write on and delivered it to him. For me, that was a sign that God was on my side.

The directors of federal parastatals wielded much power and people were afraid to approach them. I was still wondering if he delivered my note, when I saw the director hurrying out of the meeting. He led me to a nearby office and furiously demanded an explanation for interrupting his meeting. When I tried to talk, tears came gushing down my face. Somehow, I managed to explain my predicament, while asking if I was being deceived all the time, he made me wait to get the job.

While I continued talking, he turned away from my tears and faced the wall. In a voice I could not tell where it came from, I thanked him for the effort he made in assisting me. I told him that I was leaving Lagos that morning and going back home to my parents in Enugu. Jolted by my words, he swirled around. His long flowing gown swooshing with the effort and instructed me not to leave Lagos. What came next from his lips was the best news that I never anticipated;

"Come and see me on Monday morning. I will place you on contract until the embargo is lifted."

I could have hugged him in excitement, but he ran out of the room while I was jumping up and shouting - Thank you sir! while blessing him at the same time.

That was how I started the job that prepared me for a tough life. Until date, I credit my astuteness and ability to face challenges to the training I received in journalism. I worked in that television station for three years. It was a very demanding but exciting job. I absolutely enjoyed my job but with marriage, the birth of my daughter and additional responsibilities, I needed to generate more income. The salary was poor, mainly because it was a government owned establishment. I decided that the best way to survive was to move to the financial sector where I could earn more money. I applied for a customer service job in a bank and was accepted.

Planning a successful life depends on your needs and priorities. Start by understanding your environment, identifying your options, and choosing what is most suitable for your motive. Although I would have preferred to remain a journalist, a profession that gave me an opportunity to practice my love of writing and creating stories, the improved income that I received in the banking and insurance corporations I worked provided the financial power that helped to pay Adaora's school fees. I was also able to own a car, travel abroad for vacations and afford other necessities for my dependents. Work became less fun but more financially fulfilling. It was from the upgraded income that I started publishing my books. While life is all about choices, it also requires a lot of planning.

The fact is that everyone can succeed if there is a determination to do so. There can be no success without a decision, followed by a plan. Strategies must be set, objectives established, logistics taken care of before success can be achieved. Success is not something you wish for and it suddenly happens. Every successful venture was previously a dream, nurtured over a period before implementation. There is always a gestation period before it is time to reap the benefits of hard work. Success brings happiness and everyone wants to associate with a successful person.

> "THE TIME TO REPAIR THE ROOF IS WHEN THE SUN IS SHINING."
> – JOHN F. KENNEDY

LESSONS:

- Planning gives you a direction
- Your plan is your driving force
- The human mind is very strong
- Encourage your children to be independent
- You need God to open doors for you
- God gives us courage even when we are weak
- Every successful venture was previously a dream
- Dream big
- Do not give up, even when it seems impossible
- Identify your needs and set your priorities

CHAPTER 14

COMMUNICATE EFFECTIVELY

> "THE DIFFERENCE BETWEEN THE RIGHT WORD AND THE ALMOST RIGHT WORD IS THE DIFFERENCE BETWEEN LIGHTNING AND THE LIGHTING BUG" MARK TWAIN

Communication means sending or receiving information, while to communicate simply means to share or exchange information or ideas. The Oxford dictionary, in its numerous definitions of communication, includes conveying an emotion or feeling in a non-verbal way or transmitting an infectious disease, heat, or motion. However, for the purpose of this discussion, we will focus on the definition - "to share or exchange information or ideas." In every relationship or situation where you have people with a common purpose, engaged in any form of business, religious or sports related activity, who are unable to share or exchange information or ideas, you can be rest assured that it will most likely collapse.

There is no way any relationship can succeed without adequate communication. Husbands and wives need to communicate with each other. The same applies to boyfriends and girlfriends, parents and their children, teachers and students, workers, and their employers. The inability to share or exchange information or ideas is more than sufficient reason for any relationship to fail. For the success and survival of relationships, people must effectively communicate with each other. Some people assume that their partners already know what they have in mind. They are wrong. Assumption is the easiest road to wrong conclusions and eventually leads to conflicts. If you want to be understood, communicate. If you do not communicate, you have no right to blame anyone for misunderstanding you.

A major reason why there are so many unhappy homes today is because a lot of men do not communicate. They keep quiet, believing their wives or partners know everything they are thinking until something goes wrong, then they blame them for what they know nothing about. Communication makes life easier. It puts you and the next person on the same page. When someone is deprived of information, she reacts to whatever she perceives, but once she is informed, her attitude changes because she now has a better understanding of the situation.

The main reason why there are so many failed marriages in the world today is because of the inability of couples to communicate effectively. Often, the time they should have spent talking to each other and sharing ideas is spent on pursuing their individual careers, money making ventures, extended family matters and societal demands. They get so immersed in these individual pursuits that they forget to pay adequate attention to their partners, until their relationships collapse. It is always more rewarding to involve your partner in everything you are doing. That way, you are both informed, and in tune with each other's schemes.

Communication not only ensures harmony in relationships, but also builds trust. Communication is a very important tool for achieving success. Communication makes success possible. This can be achieved through talking, writing, telephone calls or e mails. You cannot succeed unless you are able to communicate. It does not matter how fantastic your ideas are, if you fail to convey and organize them properly, it is very unlikely that you will succeed.

There is no way you can carry people along with you in a project if they do not even understand what you are talking about. You should be capable of informing and convincing your project members to buy into your idea to accomplish the task. This can only be done through communication. If team members can communicate, discuss their plans and objectives, share day-to-day challenges and achievements, and review strategies, there will always be success. In such a situation where they can express their thoughts and plans to each other, learn from their team mate's mistakes and design solutions to their common problems, they will certainly achieve remarkable success. This is why communication is very important. That is perhaps why the world recently experienced an explosion in the field of communication.

Through my training in school and while working in the media, I acquired effective communication skills. This has helped tremendously in ensuring that I am always well understood. I detest ambiguity because it creates confusion. Fraudulent people are often ambiguous and very secretive. For them it is an effective tool for deception. Lack of or ineffective communication is the easiest way to destroy relationships. Therefore, learn how to say exactly what you want to say and mean every word you speak. If you do not, you have only yourself to blame when your intentions are misunderstood.

The same principle applies in business relationships where you must remain in constant touch with your clients. This enables you to obtain feedback from them regarding their transactions, understand their needs, and respond promptly to their requests. Failing to do so, may lead to being ignorant of developments that when not adequately handled will result in losing some of your valuable clients.

To understand how significant communication is to your day-to-day activities, let us examine what you do when you communicate. When you interface, you open yourself to the next person. You are indirectly saying to him- This is who I am, I am willing to trust you, which is why I am talking to you, and I want you to trust me too. Let us work together for a particular purpose, so that we can succeed. The message should be so clear and convincing that the next person understands it and is therefore able to make a choice.

He, has a right to either accept the offer or not. If he consents, he relays the same message to you, then you can begin to share and exchange information or ideas.

Always remember that for communication to contribute to success, it must be effective. To achieve your aim, the person you are relaying the information to or sharing ideas with must understand the message you are conveying. This is the main reason why it is imperative that while communicating, you should employ the simplest words. Avoid bogus words in whatever language you communicate and use only those words that the next person understands. Words are powerful.

Remember that you received the gift of words for this purpose – to communicate. The same simple but effective words you use to communicate with others are the same words you employ to talk to your creator. When praying, you should always say what you mean and mean exactly what you say. To communicate, you can choose to write the words instead of just saying them. Beyond writing and speaking, you may prefer to express your thoughts through painting, music, or drama.

I firmly believe that knowing how important it is for man to be able to communicate, God made it possible for him to use his eyes, hands, legs, and every part of his body for communication purposes. People with various kinds of disabilities are therefore still able to communicate. Have you ever wondered why the active parts of the body become even more useful when someone is unable to speak, or why it is possible to understand how someone feels by interpreting their body language?

When someone blinks at you, he is conveying a message. A child cries and his mother begins to fret because she understands that he is expressing himself. By crying, he is either requesting for food or wants to sleep. He may just be indicating that he is uncomfortable. It is possible he is simply saying-

"Please change my diaper, I am wet."

The fact is that whenever you see someone crying, he has a story to tell. Most times, it is a sad one but at other times it is a story of joy. All you probably need to do is give him a chance and you are sure to hear his story.

Since communication has become the key to solving numerous and diverse worldwide problems, it is imperative that anyone that wants to succeed should learn how to communicate. There is so much to gain from communicating and even more to benefit from doing so effectively. A child who constantly communicates with his parents hardly gets into trouble. A parent that communicates with his child gains his trust and respect. A couple that communicates with each other enjoys a happy marriage. Communication makes them trust each other, believe in each other, and remain loyal to each other.

Being aware of each other's dreams and aspirations, they are better able to plan and execute projects together. They may decide to organize their lives in such a way that they always spend their leisure time together and end up being much happier for it. A couple that communicates is a happy couple. They often entertain each other with stories about their work, family, friends, and neighbors. They are never bored. They can freely discuss issues and conveniently share ideas. It is easier for them to advice each other, whenever the need arises. They establish a lasting friendship and depend on each other for succor in times of trial. A couple that does not communicate, easily relies on friends and relatives who may not have good intentions.

Communication breaks down barriers; elicits empathy, ends wars, and establish trust. Communication is essential and should be effective.

Let us look at the following scenario. Alex comes in to see the Managing Director of a company and meets the Receptionist. The Receptionist is not the MD, but holds an important position. She is the front office staff, deliberately positioned to represent the image of the organization. Alex realizes that he must go through her before getting to his destination, which is the MD's office. She is supposed to welcome him with a smile and make sure he is comfortable until she can usher him into the MD's office. She may not be pleasantly disposed to entertaining him. It is possible she had been having a bad day or is a little bit under the weather and was unable to take the day off. The stress shows on her face as she struggles to perform her duties. Alex is coming for a very important meeting and has a confirmed appointment.

Unknown to him, his ability to hold the meeting will ultimately be determined by how courteous he is to the receptionist. If he approaches her with a superior attitude or talks to her in a patronizing manner, he just may get a rude "the MD is not around" or 'the MD is in a meeting'. Perhaps he will wait for hours and may eventually not get to see the MD, except he is wise enough to contact him directly on his private line or call his Personal Assistant. On the other hand, if he is respectful, she may not only get him into the MD's office immediately, but also become a reliable informant through whom he can henceforth obtain follow up information regarding his visit. Knowing that the last thing he wants is for the Receptionist to frustrate or constitute an obstacle for him; Alex decides to be extra polite. He is so nice that he succeeds in convincing her that the meeting is very important to him. She facilitates his meeting with her boss and provides her private line for follow up calls.

There is everything good in communicating effectively to avoid being misunderstood. By so doing, your perspective on issues will always be clear. Your team members and colleagues will know exactly what you want them to do and understand how quickly you need the task accomplished. It is only through effective communication that you can make them appreciate the need for speed and efficiency, whilst ensuring that they develop a proper grasp of the company's policies, values, and ethics. Due to the inability to communicate effectively, several departmental heads have failed in leading their team members. This inadvertently affects their relationship with their subordinates. Over time, it results in a lack of trust, inability to team properly and decline in productivity.

Communication is equally relevant in personal relationships. If you do not clearly express your thoughts, it will be difficult for the next person to understand your plans and motives. Imagine a scenario where a man sees a girl he likes and approaches her. He takes her out to dinner, spends time with her, and introduces her to his friends. He fails to inform her about his intention to have an intimate relationship with her. Another man meets the same girl, admires, and approaches her. He pays her a lot of attention, invites her out, and makes his intention known by discussing it with her. She is excited and agrees to date him. What do you think will be the reaction of the first man? Your guess is as good as mine.

When this happens, as it often does, the first man claims that he was betrayed. He blames the girl for casting him aside. He is to blame for failing to communicate his intention to her. He forgot that she has a right to choose whether to date him or not. Communication is vital because it not only affects every aspect of our day-to-day living, but also determines whether we succeed.

> "THE ART OF COMMUNICATION IS THE LANGUAGE OF LEADERSHIP."
> – JAMES HUMES

LESSONS:

- Communication makes success possible
- Assumption is the easiest road to disharmony
- Ambiguity creates confusion
- Communication builds trust
- A child who constantly communicates with his parents hardly gets into trouble

You Too Can Overcome Life's Challenges

- A parent that communicates with his child gains his trust and respect
- A couple that communicates with each other enjoys a happy marriage
- Communication breaks down barriers
- Ambiguity creates confusion
- Fraudulent people are ambiguous

CHAPTER 15

BE GENEROUS

> "TRUE GENEROSITY IS AN OFFERING, GIVEN FREELY AND OUT OF PURE LOVE. NO STRINGS ATTACHED. NO EXPECTATIONS. – SUZE ORMAN

According to the Oxford English Dictionary, the word give means to freely transfer possession of, cause to receive or have, communicate, or import, commit, consign, or entrust, cause to experience... There are other meanings attached to the word but permit me to focus on the meanings indicated above.

Help someone because you empathize with him and really want to assist. Giving, because someone needs your assistance and you genuinely want to help is exactly what we are discussing. Give only because you feel compassion for your fellow human being and not because you are expecting a reward. This is the best way to give. When you genuinely give, you are rewarded with blessings. For being compassionate, God showers his blessings upon you. When you give to someone in genuine need, you may never be able to quantify what you receive in return.

The heart of the person is full of gladness and as the recipient dances and rejoices with delight, the angels of God applaud you. The recipient often prays for his benefactor, asking God to bless and reward him. God listens and responds. This is why, each time you genuinely give, God rewards you abundantly and sometimes in such an embarrassing proportion that is incomparable to what you gave. I believe that your reward is God's way of appreciating your generosity and encouraging you.

Always remember that wealth by its nature only multiplies when you share it. If you hold on to what you have and refuse to allow others to benefit from it, one day you will wake up and it will all be gone.

You Too Can Overcome Life's Challenges

You will realize that it has been taken away from you and given to those that will dispense it according to God's plan. When you share your wealth, you distribute happiness and receive joy in return. Once people around you are happy, you will be happy. If you make them miserable by not showing concern for their welfare, you will find it difficult to even enjoy your sleep. Whether you accept it or not, when you breed unhappiness, you can never be happy. This is perhaps the main reason why despite all their riches, stingy men are miserable and often die without experiencing true happiness.

As children of God, everyone should adopt a generous attitude. God has given man the free will to choose whether to be good or bad. Everyone has the right to share joy or pain because whether we like it or not, we are all givers. When you withhold your wealth and by so doing deprive others from benefiting from your generosity, you are sharing pain and suffering. You may unintentionally invite the wrath of God who taught us how to give. Remember that God gave us life. He gave us food to eat, air to breathe. He also gave us his son Jesus Christ who lived among us and offered his life for our salvation.

We must not forget that God is always watching us. He is all seeing and all knowing. Each time we hold on to what we ought to have given out, we deprive ourselves Lack of generosity prevents us from being able to present our needs before God which limits the blessings we receive.

It is true that when we stretch out our palms to give, we receive. It is also a fact that the more we give, the more we receive. This may be why those who are generous, often prosper more than stingy people. Over the years, I have tried to understand why it is very difficult for stingy people to give out things they no longer need. Some of them try to justify their behavior by saying that no one accumulates wealth by throwing away his possessions. At every opportunity, I have tried to explain to such people that assisting others, especially those that are truly in need, does not in any way amount to throwing away someone's possessions.

God makes people wealthy so that they can share what they have acquired with the less advantaged. While it is true that some people abuse the privilege of receiving by always expecting more favors and never reaching out to assist others; it should never discourage you from being generous. The fact that some underprivileged are never grateful should also not discourage you. When you give, let it be because of God, not because you expect something in return. It is better not to expect appreciation from the people you assist so that you will not be disappointed.

Other excuses people often make for not helping the needy are; I do not have enough money, I am poor, so I cannot give. This is very wrong – no one is too poor to give. My candid advice has always been and remains; give what you have, give what you can afford, for it is better than not to give at all. I am not referring to assisting someone because you are expecting something in return or because you want to enhance your image, which is what politicians do. I am referring to giving from the heart which should be done willingly and without reservation.

Life is too short for anyone to choose to live a very wealthy life and die in a miserable way. Begin to render a helping hand to the less privileged people around you, knowing that no matter how much wealth you amass, when you die, you go with absolutely nothing.

I once witnessed a young, vibrant man sitting beside me collapse and die, within a few minutes of running into a courtroom. That incident made me realize how easily a man's life can be taken away and how powerless he becomes the moment his spirit departs from his body. Death incapacitates man. He is not even able to determine what will happen to his corpse or who will inherit his wealth. The experience led me to ask myself why man struggles so much to hold on to what he will eventually lose.

There is everything good to benefit from being generous. There is a feeling of fulfillment and inner joy that comes from assisting someone in need. I have experienced the joy of giving so many times and will share some of my encounters with you in the next three chapters. I am convinced that after reading them, you will marvel at some of the rewards I received from being generous.

LESSONS:

- Do not give because you expect something in return
- Give because you genuinely want to assist
- God rewards those who are generous
- Wealth multiplies when it is shared
- You can only be happy if you make others happy
- Joy comes from giving

CHAPTER 16

FEEDING THE HUNGRY

> "REMEMBER THAT THERE IS NO HAPPINESS IN HAVING OR IN GETTING BUT ONLY IN GIVING. REACH OUT. SHARE, SMILE, HUG, HAPPINESS IS A PERFUME THAT YOU CANNOT POUR ON OTHERS WITHOUT GETTING A FEW DROPS ON YOURSELF."
> – OG MANDINO

On a certain Saturday morning, I went to my Auto mechanic workshop to arrange for my car to be serviced. As I was driving in, I saw the apprentice who my mechanic was in the habit of sending to my house to repair my car when it needed a quick fix. His name was Kazeem. He lay on the pavement, in a fetal position. When he raised his head to acknowledge my presence, I could tell that he was hungry and probably had not eaten since morning. The sun was already up. A glance at my wristwatch confirmed that it was very close to lunchtime.

Something in his eyes convinced me that he was very hungry. Instinctively and without any form of reservation, I beckoned to him. In my wallet, I had only a Two Hundred Naira note. Sincerely, that was all the money I had, 'home and abroad' as Nigerians would say. This is a phrase used for expressing how badly broke someone is. When I handed over the money to Kazeem, I could see the transformation in his countenance. There was joy written all over his face as he thanked me profusely, bowing his head in Yoruba fashion. It was not one of my prosperous days. On the contrary, it was a season of financial challenges. I was in between jobs and had a little child to feed but the pain of hunger I saw in his eyes compelled me to assist him.

After handing over my widow's mite to Kazeem, I was overwhelmed with empathy and could not take my eyes off him. He sprang up immediately and quickly went over to a shelf in the corner where plates were stacked. He picked up a bowl and ran straight to a food stall nearby where he bought a plate of rice. He hurried back and started shoveling it into his mouth. I smiled with relief, still not taking my eyes off him. I was glad, knowing that my instincts were right about how famished he was and that I was useful to someone desperately in need. I left the workshop with absolutely no regret for parting with all I had, despite not knowing the source of our next meal.

An hour later, I received an unexpected gift. In my hand was an envelope containing the sum of Two Thousand Naira. It was given to me by a friend whom I stopped by to visit. He said that he felt that I needed money. It was such a pleasant surprise since we did not discuss my financial state. I was delighted. I knew that I was being rewarded for my kind gesture to the apprentice mechanic.

Through a friend, God had just returned tenfold what I gave out to someone in need. It was a clear reminder that God is always watching over us. He knows all our worries and our innermost thoughts. What I received was over and above what I gave out and in accordance with God's promise as it was written in the Holy Bible,

Proverbs 22:9;

"A generous man will himself be blessed for he shares his food with the poor."

I received much more than that money. Whenever my car needed minor repairs and Kazeem's boss sent him to me, he eagerly worked on it. Each time I watched him working on my car, I noticed that he would be smiling like a little boy playing with his favorite toy. I knew that I had his goodwill which made me feel appreciated and loved.

There is absolutely nothing to lose from helping someone in need, rather there is a lot to gain. Day in day out, we have in our midst, the rich who ignore the plight of the downtrodden, unknowingly committing sins of omission. They drive past them on the streets, pretending that they do not exist. May we all strive not to be like the rich man in the Holy Bible book of Luke 16: 19 - 31 - who although he saw Lazarus, the leper, crying for help, ignored him.

You Too Can Overcome Life's Challenges

LESSONS:

- Give because you feel compassion, not because you expect a reward
- Wealth multiplies only when you share it
- If you make people happy, you will be happy
- God blesses us so that we can share with the less privileged
- Generosity breeds goodwill

CHAPTER 17

A GOOD MAN'S BURIAL

> "WHAT WE HAVE DONE FOR OURSELVES DIES WITH US,
> WHAT WE HAVE DONE FOR OTHERS AND THE WORLD
> REMAINS AND IS IMMORTAL"
> – ALBERT PIKE

Another remarkable experience I had which also made me realize how benevolent God is and the fantastic reward that comes with the act of giving, was during my late father's burial. Let me first tell you a little about my father and give you an insight into the role he played in the society before he died. My father was Chief Godwin Ukeje Ndiolo who died at a known age of 83. My grandparents were illiterate and did not actually know his date of birth. He therefore had to select a date he believed was appropriate.

He was a man who had a lot of faith in hard work, service to God and to humanity. He was a very intelligent man who served Nigeria with all his heart. He studied in the United Kingdom where he was awarded a first degree in Economics and a Master's degree in Business Management. He was a very passionate man to Mary Magdalene his wife and to us, his children. He was also a great disciplinarian. We gained so much knowledge and wisdom from him that most of us became exemplary children. We learned more about the principles of good living from him than we learned from all our teachers. In addition, he taught us to always remember where we came from, to be proud of who we are and to fear no man but God. He was a selfless man. He was always willing to defend his family, friends, relatives, and other members of our community. He was a very generous man.

He was so reliable and responsible that he was recognized and honored with the title of, Ochendo in my local dialect, which means an umbrella. My father was someone my siblings and I had grown to love and respect so much that the memories of our years with him will live forever in our hearts. He was someone we all relied upon whenever we needed counsel on any subject. Regrettably, after a prolonged battle with prostate cancer and pneumonia, we lost him on November 24, 2003.

He lived a fulfilled life and therefore deserved an appropriate burial. He needed to receive what my people refer to as "a befitting burial." Unfortunately, the onus rested on me to ensure that his burial was successful. I was not his first child. I was the fourth female child in a family of nine children. Three of my sisters, including the first-born child of my parents were living in the United States. My mother was also in the United States. Although I had an elder sister that was local, for reasons best known to my father, just before he died, he chose me to organize his burial. He was on admission in a hospital in Enugu, when my mother called and said that he wanted to speak with me. My father was a straightforward kind of man who said exactly what he meant, without mincing words.

On that day, his words were shrouded in ambiguity – "Gay- Gay, (as he fondly called me, which was my family pet name from my baptismal name Gertrude) if something happens, do not wait for anyone. Take the bull by the horns and do what you must do." As uncanny as it may sound, that was how my father placed the responsibility of organizing his burial squarely on my shoulders. This was shortly before he passed on. Initially, I had no clear idea what he was talking about. First, I was a female child and I was not the first female (the Ada in my local language). I was the fourth female child.

My father was a very assertive man whose instructions were always carried out by us. I did not dwell on his words and had forgotten about it before he died. It was when I saw his corpse, that the true meaning of what he said struck me. It was difficult for me to accept that he was gone. After shaking him vigorously, thinking that I could rouse him back to life, without success, it finally dawned on me that my insurmountable father has been defeated by death. A great man has gone to rest.

I began to organize his burial with my personal resources and with as much contribution as I could gather from my sisters. I had a definite picture of the way his burial should be and concentrated on planning it. Family meetings were held, where prevailing issues were resolved.

Logistics and modalities were agreed upon. There remained the issue of raising funds for his burial. This became a huge challenge. It was rather difficult to raise the amount of money required for my father's burial. My father had long retired from civil service, had no insurance and no money saved up for his burial. Besides, my parents had eight daughters and one son. Female children were considered irrelevant at that time and some people believed that we did not have the funds required to perform the kind of elaborate ceremony for burying a man of his status.

I prayed for divine assistance. There was an instant turn around. My financial state improved tremendously. I spent all that was within my disposal without calculating how much of my personal funds were involved. Monetary contributions were made by my siblings and I ensured that they were utilized for the burial. It was a very difficult period. We called on God to see us through and he responded in a way that was beyond our expectations. What earlier seemed so difficult became a reality. My father's burial was so magnificent that it became a point of reference by our relatives, members of our community and friends, years after he died.

We were later informed that some of our relatives were expecting us to come pleading for assistance from them. We did not and they were astonished at the graceful way my father was buried. It was made possible by divine assistance.

Through God's intervention, every aspect of my father's burial was successful. From the procurement of his casket, to the cost of transporting twelve pallbearers from a famous funeral parlor in Lagos to our village in Oma - Eke, Enugu state, God made everything we desired available for his burial ceremony. This was because we wanted; with all our hearts to give our father a befitting burial, despite our limited resources.

I recall that it all started from the moment I walked into the funeral parlor where I was to select a casket for my father. A feeling of helplessness overwhelmed me at the realization that my father whom I loved so much was gone, overwhelmed me. At the sight of the beautifully designed caskets displayed in their show room, tears ran down my face. Transfixed, I stood, staring at the caskets, tears of sorrow filled my eyes. I was silently asking myself repeatedly what I was doing in a funeral parlor. I should never have been the one selecting a casket for my late father, but I had no choice. It was supposed to have been the duty of a male member of my family. In my tradition, the men were ordained the rightful heads of families and assumed to be stronger. It was such a difficult thing to do. How was I to select a casket for someone I loved so deeply, to bury him? I had no idea that I was being observed.

The Director of the funeral home was a very kind man. One of his workers may have called his attention to me, a distraught lady in their office. He came into the display room and ushered me to his office where he offered me a seat. He began to console me, saying that he understood how I felt. It was clear that he was used to helping bereaved people deal with the difficult task of selecting caskets suitable for burying their loved ones. He displayed a lot of compassion while helping me to select a beautiful casket for my father. It was a white casket, made with a glass top and solid wood on the sides. Unfortunately, I cannot mention his name since I could not obtain his permission to do so before he died in a very unfortunate plane crash. I will also not mention the name of his organization for the same reason but will always be grateful to him.

Although it was exactly what I would have selected for my father's burial, I rejected it because it was over and above my family's budget. He was very patient with me. He made me feel comfortable by listening to the beautiful stories I told about my late father's life and achievements. When I hesitated, he urged me on and even asked some questions about the great man I was talking about. He seemed genuinely interested in how much love and respect I had for my father. He showed so much interest in my father's accomplishments that he made me feel much better.

When I finished, he consoled me with the most appropriate words. Then to my utter delight, he promised that his organization will provide the casket and carry out all the burial requirements at a huge discount. I was dumbfounded and cried some more. He left me in his office to grieve in private and went to attend to other matters. When he returned, I thanked him profusely. He said that he decided to help me because he could perceive that deep within my heart, I genuinely wanted to give my father a befitting burial. He felt that my desire was purely out of love and not because I wanted to impress anyone.

Although I was surprised that he could see through me, his perception of my motive was right.

I had always known that I had a special relationship with my late father. Apart from our both being highly principled disciplinarians, we had similar interests. This became more glaring to me as I blossomed into adulthood. I found myself reading the same books he read and travelling to some of the countries he visited when he was much younger. I will never forget how excited my father was when he learned that I had just returned from Ghana. This was after my first trip to Kwame Nkrumah's country. I also remember how joyously he received the beautiful and brightly colored Kente shirt I bought for him. He sat with me and recounted tales of his visit to Ghana. That was shortly before he succumbed to the cold and brutal hands of death.

I and my father shared lots of beautiful moments together. There were days when I danced for him and when we danced together. I was completely devastated when he died. The Funeral Director's words were like a cooling balm on my exhausted nerves. He was like an angel sent by God to help me through a very difficult moment that I was not in any way prepared for.

His words brought me the much-desired solace I needed and after that day I could feel God's hands working out my father's burial for me.

When I narrated my encounter with the Funeral Director to my family members, they were ecstatic. Some of my siblings were skeptical. They were wondering if he was going to fulfill his promise. To everyone's great delight, he did everything he promised. He made our sorrow lighter in a very special way. Up until this day, every member of my family remembers his kindness. Due to his generosity, my father's burial was like a carnival. We were able to achieve what previously seemed like an improbable dream. He sent twelve pallbearers to accompany my father's casket from Lagos all the way to our hometown in Oma -Eke in Enugu state for the burial ceremony.

For three days, the pall bearers lodged in a hotel in Enugu, at no extra cost to me and my family. I still feel indebted to him and will never forget what he did for us. I am convinced that my father and all the other souls whose families he assisted in such desperate circumstances would have welcomed him to heaven with wide smiles on their lips.

You Too Can Overcome Life's Challenges

Regrettably, he may never realize how much his generosity meant to my family because he died without having a chance to read this book.

There are many lessons to learn from the experience I had at the Undertakers. Had I not taken some bold steps; I may not have even met the man that God used to favor me. Secondly, I could have looked at the caskets, decided that they were too expensive, and walked away without dreaming or wishing that I could afford them. When the director took me to his office, I may not have started talking to him about my father. I believe that everything that happened was pre destined. My father was a very generous man who did everything he could to help a lot of people while he was alive. He assisted widows, sponsored the education of many people and placed others in jobs. Many of the people he assisted were at his burial to honor him.

It pays to be real. Whatever situation you are facing, be yourself. It also pays to be bold, as Ben Franklin said – "Nothing ventured, nothing gained." Even if you do not know how you are going to achieve what you are dreaming about, take a step towards that direction. Do not just sit back and procrastinate. The saying that 'heaven helps those who help themselves' is true.

Apart from being generous with your finances, be generous with your time. Time is one of the greatest gifts to give to another person. We all have things to do and targets to meet. Increasingly, I have discovered that making out time to dedicate to assisting other people in need is very difficult. When you do so, be sure that you will be rewarded. All you need to do is look around you and you will see many people in need. It may be an elderly person trying to cross a road or a little child that is lost and trying to find his way home. It may even be someone at a grocery store who cannot afford to pay for his groceries or someone that just needs a listening ear. Do your best to help as much as you can.

It is very important to try and perform your duty, even when you feel inadequate. God was with me throughout my late father's burial. He continued to shower his blessings upon me in an amazing way even after I returned to my place of residence in Lagos. It was the same year that I buried my father that I was able to buy a plot of land in Lagos and travelled on my first business trip to Dubai.

LESSONS:

- God knows all your worries and innermost thoughts
- What you teach your children lives with them forever
- God never gives you responsibilities you cannot handle
- Be kind to people in distress
- Do things for the right reasons
- It pays to be real
- Always be willing to help others

CHAPTER 18

SAVING THE DYING BIRD

TO PRACTICE FIVE THINGS UNDER ALL CIRCUMSTANCES
CONSTITUTES PERFECT VIRTUE; THESE FIVE ARE
GRAVITY, GENEROSITY OF SOUL, SINCERITY,
EARNESTNESS, AND KINDNESS." - CONFUCIUS

I had just finished seeing off a guest with Chima, a close friend of mine, when I noticed a bird that fell into our garden. It lay helplessly on its side. I signaled to Chima and we moved closer to take a better look. Chima and I were like minds; two creative and adventurous people. We noticed that the bird was injured. It was bleeding. The little bird lay precariously on its side, gasping for breath. It had lost some blood and was so weak that it could not even stand. Without a word to each other, we picked it up, took it into a shade, found a small box with an opening for air, and placed it inside. Although we had no experience in caring for animals and had no idea exactly what to do with a wounded bird, we simply followed our instincts.

Deciding that it might have been dehydrated, we opened its beak and with the help of a little cup gently poured water down its throat. As the water cascaded down its throat, the bird stirred with a welcome relief and drank more water. We watched with fascinating interest, convinced that we took the right step Then, it shut its eyes and was motionless. We were scared, thinking it was dead, then realized with relief that it had started breathing slowly. We made sure that it was very comfortable, left it to rest for a while and went into the house.

Hours later, 1 came out to check on our friend, and was alarmed to find an empty space inside the box. For a moment, I stood still, trying to figure out what could have happened to our little friend. While helping the bird we had somehow become fond of it. Slowly, it dawned on me that having gathered sufficient energy, it must have flown back to wherever it came from. My cheerful cry of joy got Chima running out of the house. We danced around together celebrating our dear friend's recovery and successful return to the sky.

You cannot begin to imagine our happiness for being able to save a helpless bird that was on the verge of losing its precious life. We marveled at the realization that water, shelter, as well as compassion were all the bird needed to survive an impending death. We felt very good with ourselves for playing the role of angels sent to rescue the wounded bird. We celebrated the bird's full recovery, knowing that somewhere up in the sky lived a very grateful bird. When you see someone or an animal in need, do not walk away. Instead, do something to help. You just may be its only chance for survival.

I am totally convinced that it pays to be kind and generous. Some years ago, I met an exceptionally rich man who was so kind that everyone that encountered him benefitted from his magnanimity. He oversaw one of the government parastatals and had a lot of money at his disposal. This man's character was completely different from that of many people in his position. Instead of being corrupt and arrogant, he was kind and humble. He gave freely to his friends, relatives, co -workers, churches, and many people that met him. He had such a generous aura that I concluded that it was the generosity of his heart that clearly reflected on him. I could not help but imagine the number of prayers being said for him by grateful hearts. For someone who did a lot of good and earned tremendous goodwill, he received many blessings in return for his kindness. He was very rich.

For me, the most amazing aspect of this kind hearted man was his humility and simplicity. He had such an unassuming personality. He wore the simplest of clothes; T-shirts on Jeans trousers, palm sandals or flip- flops on his feet. He was so humble that judging by his looks, someone could easily dismiss him for an inconsequential man. I found his humility so intriguing and respected him much more for it.

I am not saying that it is not a good thing to receive. It is more rewarding and more honorable to give than to receive. Giving is a win-win situation. When you give, you lose nothing, rather all you have given and much more eventually returns to you. Let us learn to be generous. The world is so full of pain and anguish because people have not learned how to love one another. When you give love, it returns to you. It is important to be selfless in giving and to do so without reservation. When you give, you experience the true joy that comes from being generous.

If you want to succeed, be generous and learn how to accommodate others. Be kind to people that you live and work with. Be helpful to those that need assistance, even when they do not specifically approach you. Show that you care about others and always share what you have. If you are generous with your time and money, you will be surprised how quickly you recover what you spent. Also, get involved in serving your community both at home and in church. Offer your services for free, the benefits you will derive from doing so will surprise you. By helping others, you are indirectly doing yourself a favor.

When the people you have helped pray for you, the heavens open and blessings come showering down upon you. An inexplicable inner joy is derived from helping people in genuine need. Spend time with less privileged people. Make out time to visit orphanages, hospitals and physically or mentally challenged homes. When you go on such visits, please take your family with you. Children learn a lot from visiting such homes. These acts of love will humble you all and make you appreciate what God has been doing for your family.

It is common knowledge that the richest people in the world are often acknowledged as being very generous. It is also true that the more you give, the more you receive. Money is not meant to be confined; it was designed to be shared and used as a symbol of exchange. Sharing what you have, gives you more. It gives you joy, peace and a feeling of accomplishment. There is also no better feeling than that of watching the expression of gratitude on the faces of the people you assist. Generosity includes appreciating and complimenting people around you. Do not be stingy with compliments. There are always people who are trying to develop themselves and they need encouragement. You can assist by mentoring some of them.

LESSONS:

- When you give love, it returns to you
- When you see someone or an animal in need, do not walk away
- Spend time with the less privileged people
- When you are generous with your time and money, you will be surprised how quickly you recover what you spent
- Encourage people with your words

CHAPTER 19

BE HEALTH CONSCIOUS

"GOOD HEALTH IS A DUTY TO YOURSELF, TO YOUR
CONTEMPORARIES, TO YOUR INHERITORS, TO THE
PROGRESS OF THE WORLD
– GWENDOLYN BROOKS

If you want to live a long and fulfilled life, love yourself and take good care of your body. Whilst nourishing your soul with the word of God, take good care of yourself. Eat a balanced diet. Exercise regularly. Eat lots of fruits and vegetables. Stay hydrated by drinking water. Two or three glasses of water, first thing in the morning help in purifying your system. Go for frequent medical checkup. This should at least be carried out once a year. When you are ill, avoid self-medication. Go to a good hospital where the doctors will conduct tests before administering medication. If you are not satisfied with the diagnosis, please look for a better alternative. When in doubt, a second opinion always helps. Your health is your responsibility and to be successful, you need to be healthy.

Hospitals are filled with sick people whose priority is to get well, not work or make money. You can only think of making money when you are healthy. Remember, health is wealth. These days it is very easy to find a well-equipped gym. You can also browse the internet to find exercises you can do in the comfort of your home to keep healthy. There is everything good to benefit from exercising daily. When you work out daily, you keep your blood circulating, reduce aches and pains, have more energy for your work and invariably achieve more. If you cannot exercise every day, try and do so at least three times a week.

When I got into the habit of exercising, I realized that any day I failed to exercise I felt tired and sluggish and could barely wait for the next day to make up for it. The next day's work out was often more tasking. As I continue to exercise, it becomes easier. I feel less stressed at work and more energized. I also accomplish a lot more. Ever since I realized how important it is to stay healthy, I make the necessary sacrifice required by choosing to eat and drink healthy. No matter how delicious the dish may be, I do not over indulge. I had always known that exercising was a good habit. I had parents that said so all the time. My father made us take walks while we were kids. My father would rather walk than drive and my mother was a sports mistress. She continued exercising even in her eighties.

Exercising and dieting make you healthy, make your clothes fit better and make you feel good with yourself. Keeping fit builds confidence. If you want to succeed, you must learn how to stay healthy. The social media has made it easier to find ways of keeping fit. All you need to do is check Instagram, Facebook or TikTok and you will find very interesting options of exercises that you can do daily. Google and You tube are also easy ways to watch useful and encouraging videos. All that is required from you is the willingness to dedicate 30 minutes of your day to healthy activities that add value to your wellbeing.

The truth is that you must master how to take care yourself before you can take care of anyone else. If you are ill, you can be of little or no use to anyone. Your health and that of your friends and family matter a great deal and go a long way in determining their success as well as yours. Make it your goal to stay healthy. You can achieve it.

LESSONS:

- Exercise regularly
- Eat healthy
- Stay hydrated
- Go for your annual medical checkup

CHAPTER 20

DEATH TRAPS

"OUR LIVES BEGIN TO END THE DAY WE BECOME SILENT ABOUT THINGS THAT MATTER" - MARTIN LUTHER KING JR.

I have always been conscious of my health and would rather check into a hospital than buy medication across the counter of any pharmacy. I also exercise regularly. Unfortunately, I had the misfortune of spending five very unpleasant days on admission in a hospital in Lagos. At the end of my stay there my experience was so terrible that I concluded that Nigerian hospitals are huge death traps. Some of the doctors are unreliable. I say this with due apologies to a few doctors and nurses you and I may know who have what I call 'the true calling' for their profession. By this, I am referring to those that really go out of their way to sacrifice their time, energy, and expertise to treat the sick. They genuinely nurture pregnant women from conception, through antenatal, to delivery. These ones, whom I refer to as the 'real doctors,' will always have my sincere respect and admiration. Such doctors can be found in various other fields apart from gynecology. They truly care about their patients and understand that their job is to save lives.

I was sick for two weeks and in those weeks had been in and out of the same hospital, receiving treatment as an outpatient. I was struck with what the doctor described as multiple resistant malaria. In the first week of noticeable symptoms, the doctor I initially consulted gave me a full dose of malaria drugs. I took four tablets every morning and night for five days. They were yellow tablets and not in any way pleasing to the eyes. They made me feel worse every time I took them. Eager to get back on my feet, I swallowed them diligently. I wanted to get well as quickly as possible. I had so much to do that I considered being ill a hindrance to my success. Being an upbeat kind of person,

I have always had low tolerance for illness and needed to recover as quickly as possible.

Within those five days, I continued to go to work. I was not prepared to let malaria win the battle by preventing me from carrying on with my daily activities. Instead of feeling better, my situation worsened. By the end of that week, I returned to the same hospital.

I had to undergo lab tests to confirm if it was only malaria or with typhoid infection. The doctor prescribed additional medications for me. He combined two potent drugs and granted me three days off work. He said that I needed to rest for the treatment to be effective. The dosage of one of the drugs was three tablets, to be taken once daily for five days, while that of the second one was two tablets every day, for seven days. As is usually the case, Pain relieving medication was included. I eagerly gulped down the drugs as indicated on the transparent sachets, believing that I was on my way to recovery. I also tried my very best to rest by staying home for the recommended days, although I spent the better part of the first day at work before leaving for the clinic. I may be wrong, but I still find it difficult to understand why employers regard the very day a patient visits the hospital as one of the sick times off. This is regardless of whether the patient spends most of the day in the hospital going in and out of the doctor's office and running tests.

Despite all the medications, instead of feeling better, I felt worse. Preceding the sickness, I had gone on a ten-day trip to the United Kingdom where I was unable to visit the salon to wash my hair. I was too weak to go to the salon. I arranged for home service. The stylist washed my hair and started braiding it around 7.30pm. I was very restless and could hardly sit still. Although she was only doing cornrows, I was barely able to tolerate it. Cold and trembling with fever, I drank cups of Lipton tea with peppermint. I turned off the fan, but still could not bear the cold. She noticed how restless I was and expressed concern by continuously empathizing with me.

She was so worried that immediately she left my house, she called Annie, a close friend of mine through whom I had engaged her service and said in adulterated or broken English;

"Make you call your friend o! She no well"

Annie was upset with me for stubbornly resuming work when it was obvious that I was still recovering from the illness that she refused to call me. She had always seen me as a workaholic. Around 2.30am the following morning, when all efforts to sleep failed, I called Annie. That night was one of the worst nights that I ever had. I spent it mostly turning and tossing on my bed and could not sleep. Although the fan and air conditioner in my room were turned off, I shivered all through the night. I was feeling dizzy and very weak. My head was throbbing and the fever sapped away whatever strength that was left in me. I tried calling my next-door neighbor and his wife but their lines were switched off. I picked up my rosary and began to pray that God would keep me alive until daybreak. When the situation worsened, I panicked and called my doctor. He advised me to take two tablets of the prescribed fever and pain-relieving tablets. I eventually slept off for about two hours. I got up at 7 am, showered and went back to the hospital.

After further tests, I was astonished to learn that all the medications I gulped down for two weeks had no effect on the level of malaria parasite in my blood. As the doctor succinctly put it, "it didn't even shift at all." He decided to place me on admission and treat it intravenously, using quinine. Thus, began my five-day sojourn at the Caro Medical Centre (not the real name). Since I desperately needed to get well, I surrendered myself to their professional expertise. Let me explain here that before that desperate battle with the malaria parasite, I had never been one to easily succumb to illness. A fact which a certain nurse aptly observed;

"Madam, it has been long since you were sick" and to which I responded;

"Yes, my dear"

By my understanding, it implied that my predicament was as perplexing to the medical personnel as it was to me. The malaria parasite was so stubborn that it chose to remain in my blood stream, despite every effort to destroy it, hence the doctor's decision to" flush it out."

Before they could start the intravenous treatment, they had to scale through a hurdle. They needed to confirm the level of the infection with another blood test. My veins are very tricky. They are veins that phlebotomy technicians can see, but once they attempt to insert a needle, disappear in such a baffling way. Collecting my blood sample or fixing an IV fluid for me was always a great challenge for medical staff. Usually, there would be several attempts before any phlebotomist succeeds in locating my vein.

The journey usually starts from the most elusive veins within my elbow joint, to my wrist and then to the back of my hands. Flinching and moaning in pain, I winced, at every attempt. By the time they were through, whatever symptoms that first brought me to the hospital would have intensified. During most visits to the lab, I often try to spare myself from this recurring agony by advising the phlebotomists on the easiest place to find my veins. They ignore my advice and continue searching until they strike a suitable vein. They always perceive my discomfort as an attempt by a difficult patient to avoid their fervent needles. They were right in a way because I detest needles. They cause me a lot of pain. Their continuous poking and refusal to listen to my advice made the process more painful. My anguish was genuine and I am sure that there are many other people with tricky veins who suffer like me. It will be a great relief to patients if doctors, nurses, as well as lab technicians can listen to them. Everyone knows and understands exactly how his body works.

Fifteen minutes later, having confirmed that the level of the malaria parasite in my system was disturbingly high, the doctor concluded the admission process and I was transferred to a private room.

What happened within the next few days reminded me so much of years gone by, when I was on admission in a prestigious hospital on Victoria Island. The hospital had a chef that dressed up like the head chef in a restaurant with a remarkable cap. He was always in a vibrant mood. He used to come to my room, shortly after breakfast to ask what I would prefer for lunch and dinner. There were sumptuous options and he willingly served whatever I selected in a very cheery mood. Unknown to him, although I appreciated his effort in trying to make patients like myself happy, I felt like he was trivializing the pain that I was going through with his over cheery mood. One day, I could not hold back anymore. I asked him if he thought that he was working in a hotel. I made him realize that if I wanted to feel like I was in a hotel, I would have checked into one. He quickly got the message and apologized. Subsequently, he made every effort to approach me with sufficient empathy.

The room that I was occupying occupying was a different kind of room. Although it was supposed to be a private room with special facilities, it was sparsely furnished. It had a bed, two armchairs, bed table (the type that a patient could wheel around his bedside), shelves and a television. There was also a toilet and bathroom attached to the room. There was no refrigerator, and the television was an old box with no option of channels. Before a nurse came in to set up the intravenous infusions that the doctor prescribed, I quickly inspected the bathroom and found out that there was no toilet paper. I quickly pressed the call bell and requested for toilet paper and a soap. The nurse was quick to inform me that the hospital was not supposed to provide soap for me. I wondered how I would have coped if I had not already sent for my toiletries from home.

When it was time for lunch, the chef came by to take my order. Typically, she was donning a white dress. To my surprise, there was only one item on their menu – eba and egusi soup (fermented cassava flakes made with hot water and melon soup). There was no option. Although I knew that I needed to eat before taking any of the injection or tablets, the doctor prescribed for me, eba also known as garri with egusi soup could never have been my choice. I had not eaten garri in so many years. My eyesight was bad and since I heard that garri was not good for my eyes, I stopped eating it. I politely informed her that I was not going to eat eba and she offered to substitute it with wheat flour molded in hot water. No fruit was provided with the meal. For dinner the cook served moi – moi (made from beans) and Nigerian pap (made from corn and prepared with boiled water). In the morning, breakfast was bread, omelet, and tea. There was no other option and no fruit. Convinced that I was in serious trouble, I ate the food. My metabolism was very slow. I was often constipated. I also had symptoms of pile. The last thing I needed was a clogged stomach.

I was seriously perplexed. I could never understand why a hospital that should know the relevance of proper nutrition to the well-being of their patients did not include fruits and vegetables in their menu. The only resemblance to vegetable that I was served were little pieces of pumpkin leaves swimming on the surface of the melon soup. In my normal inquisitive manner, I demanded an explanation. The cook informed me that there was no provision made by the hospital management for fruits and vegetables to be served to patients.

Considering how handsomely the hospital charged their patients, I was very disappointed. I made calls and arranged for a daily supply of fruits and vegetables. That was the only way to ensure that I could move my bowels as often as was necessary.

While enduring the discomfort of the hospital, I could not help but notice that the house keeping staff was as unprofessional as the hospitality staff engaged by some corporate organizations. They were either completely ignorant of the real meaning of the word cleaning or preferred to make a show of their job due to inadequate supervision. I watched as they came in with their long brooms to sweep the floor. Petrified, I gaped at them as they used filthy, brownish colored, wet mops and followed the same rhythm as the broom. They cleaned the bathroom and toilet with the same nonchalant attitude as my room, not mindful of all the germs blooming there. In my frail state, there was no way I could pee without sitting on the toilet. Nothing else was cleaned. I regretted not bringing my toilet wipes or spray, which would have taken care of most of the germs.

They ignored the table and every other piece of furniture in the room. Although there were giant cobwebs looming above anyone that attempted to walk into the bathroom, there was no attempt to remove them. The tiles on the walls were untouched. No cleaning agent or disinfectant was used until the fourth day of my stay in that hospital. It was on that glorious day that the housekeeping staff mercifully changed my bed sheets for the first time since I was admitted.

I was still celebrating the clean bed sheets, while waiting for the nurse to remove the needle inserted to my left hand so that I could shower properly when the housekeeper asked if I had showered. She advised that when I finish showering, that I should ring the call bell for her colleague on afternoon duty to come and clean up. When the afternoon shift housekeeper arrived, she started arguing that her colleague on night duty must have cleaned the bathroom. I tried persuading her but she was adamant until a nurse advised her to clean the bathroom. Surprisingly, she walked in with a bucket containing many types of cleaning agents, including Harpic, my eyes sprang wide open. Oh! I muttered silently to myself. That was how I realized that the disinfectants were available but the housekeepers were just not using them.

Lost in thought and fantasizing about finally having a clean bathroom, I almost missed the sight of the housekeeper departing until she announced that she was done. I was shocked because she spent precisely five minutes. I stared at her, speechless, before collapsing on my bed. That was when I finally gave up on them.

Being the kind of person that would give anything for a clean environment, my dislike for filth and all kinds of disorderliness always got the better of me. If I was not so weak and if the hospital authorities kept the cleaning agents inside the bathroom, I would personally have cleaned that bathroom. The toilet continued to stink so much that I had to send for a can of room deodorizer to help reduce the stench. As soon as the doctors on ward round arrived, I made sure to engage them in a discussion in which I expressed my views on their unhealthy menu and the risk it posed on the health of their patients. One of their most senior consultants was leading the team.

Seemingly surprised, he insisted that there was an instruction given to the kitchen staff that vegetables and fruits must be part of their menu. It became a bit difficult for me to decide where to place the blame for the hospital's pathetic meal plan. Left to wonder why the kitchen staff refused or forgot to carry out such an important instruction, I was rescued from my dilemma when one of them came to express appreciation for my taking up the matter with their doctors. Her exact words were - "we have been asking for the money to buy fruits and vegetables, but they won't give us." I became further convinced that she was right when the menu remained the same until I was discharged from the hospital. There was no fruit or vegetable in their meals until I left.

If you think that what you just read was my worst encounter with a Nigerian hospital, you are wrong. A year earlier, I had a near death experience in a hospital in Lagos Island where a doctor prescribed an overdose of hypertensive medication for me. Experiencing symptoms of malaria, I reported at the hospital for treatment. When I went in to check my vital signs, the nurse found out that my blood pressure was slightly high. After carrying out further investigations, the doctor on duty prescribed some sedatives. He requested that I should return in a week's time to check my progress. By the time I returned, she was off duty and I had to see another doctor.

He checked my file and decided to place me on ten milligrams of a hypertensive medication, with the instruction to take one tablet twice daily. Being an ideal patient and without anticipating the lurking danger, I went home and took the meds as instructed. That night, I was so disturbed that I could not sleep. I had no idea why I was feeling very faint and dizzy. After breakfast, I took the blood pressure medication again and continued with my duties at the office. Although I felt terrible, I continued working. I went for an appointment with a client of mine and was at her office when I suddenly started feeling dizzy. I requested for some water, drank a bit of it, vomited, and passed out. When I regained consciousness, I was already at the hospital.

The doctor asked if I was on any medication. When I showed him the medication that was prescribed by the other doctor, he shouted;

"My God! Who gave you these drugs? Are you hypertensive? You are not. Even if you are, this is an overdose"

That was when I realized that I just survived death. I was placed on an intravenous therapy to flush out the hypertensive medication and stabilize my system. The doctor emphasized that I was very fortunate to have survived. The over dose crashed my blood pressure beyond an acceptable level which may have led to either death or paralysis, neither of which happened to me. I remained in that hospital for three days until my system normalized. When I was discharged everyone that heard the story advised that I should take the hospital to court and prosecute them for misconduct but I declined. Knowing Nigeria and the way the judicial system drags on for years due to high level of corruption, I decided not to engage in a legal battle. Instead of wasting precious time on an unending legal tussle that may end up dismissed or favoring the guilty party, I chose to spend that time thanking God for saving my life. The experience left me in perpetual fear of Nigerian hospitals. I decided that it was the last time I would allow myself to be used as a guinea pig by doctors in Nigerian.

Stories are rife of patients collapsing after taking medications prescribed by their doctors. I have concluded that it is important to always seek a second opinion before taking any strong medication. Life is too fragile and there is no guarantee of a second chance. Many people have died from wrong diagnosis, while several others are known to have developed more severe complications after consulting such doctors.

In the year 2001, a doctor in a reputable hospital decided that I was having heart issues which he described as palpitations of the heart. He prescribed several medications for me. I went through a difficult period in my life in which I believed that my life was coming to an end. I decided not to give up without a fight. I consulted four different doctors in various parts of Nigeria, spending a lot of money and working with them to find a solution. I changed my diet and lifestyle and started avoiding all forms of stress. Initially, I believed that I was consulting professionals who were sure of what they were doing. I spent more money on echocardiogram and stress tests that the doctors recommended to confirm the status of my heart. This went on until I was able to travel to California where I consulted another doctor. After going through observation and tests, he concluded that there was nothing wrong with my heart. Interestingly, the doctor was a Nigerian doctor living in the United States.

My mother's experience also did nothing to allay my reservations for consulting doctors in Nigeria. While in Nigeria, she was being treated for waist pain, arthritis, heart problems, and chest pain for years, without any of her doctors realizing that she was diabetic. In 2004 when she first visited the United States, she went to a hospital there and the doctor discovered that she had been diabetic for years. Her sugar level was so high that she was on the verge of having a stroke when she arrived the United States. The doctor informed her that she was lucky she was diagnosed at the eleventh hour.

It is a big shame that with all the intelligent doctors, nurses and well-trained medical personnel in Nigeria, hospitals are not functioning like professional medical establishments. Nigerians keep demanding reliable health care from their leaders who prefer to travel outside the country for medical care instead of fixing the dilapidated medical facilities in the country.

People continue to die on daily basis from child birth complications. Many other lives are lost from malaria, typhoid fever and other illnesses because of wrong diagnoses and poor medical facilities. The situation is so disturbing that many Nigerians suffering from prostate cancer and who can afford to travel abroad, find their way to India, United Kingdom, Germany, South Africa, or Ghana for surgery.

Pregnant women carry their unborn children to full term, afraid of delivery complications. This has led to churches offering special prayers for their safe delivery. Many hospitals function without incubators for pre mature babies, while others do not have machines for oxygen therapy. Should you require oxygen in such hospitals, you are doomed. That was the case with my younger sister Kate who was hooked up to an obsolete oxygen machine that was empty until she died. The same applies to being transfused with blood from their so - called blood banks. Some patients that received blood from Nigerian hospitals end up with infection. The medical equipment in many hospitals in Nigeria are outdated.

It is sad to note that Nigerian supervisory bodies that approve these hospitals and are supposed to ensure that they are well equipped fail to do so. So much has been written in the newspapers regarding schools from where Nigerian doctors qualify. I have even heard that some of the Universities offer admission to more students than they have the capacity to train. Consequently, the doctors graduate without being quite prepared for the enormous responsibility ahead of them.

To put an end to the death of innocent citizens in the hands of such doctors, it is time to begin to ask some relevant questions; why should the Nigerian government continue to allow non-accredited universities to offer medicine? Why are such "doctors" allowed to sit for the assessment exam, which if they scale through by whatever means, certifies them to practice medicine in Nigeria. Why do Nigerians continue to ignore the situation and keep gambling their lives away? I am writing this not because I am interested in indicting anyone, but with the hope that the relevant authorities will finally wake up to their responsibilities and begin to take appropriate measures required to save lives.

I honestly believe that the case of the Nigerian health sector is not peculiar. Rather, it reflects other aspects of the economy like education, commerce, and industry. I am focusing on the health sector because it has become an area of major concern to most citizens of Nigeria. Everyone, from the lower to the middle class, including the super-rich visit these hospitals when the need arises. The politicians and super rich, who travel to developed countries for medical care, occasionally use the local hospitals when there is an emergency. When critically examined, most of the challenges faced by Nigerian hospitals are corruption based.

While it is obvious that Nigeria can afford to provide well-equipped hospitals for its citizens, there has not been an adequate effort to do so. Unfortunately, the leadership of Nigeria continues to toy with sectors like health and education which are considered crucial for development in other countries.

For hospitals, restoration of their patients to good state of body and mind is the reason why they exist. It is therefore expected that they should be capable of doing so. This should be the first consideration for any one selecting a hospital instead of concentrating on how nicely painted the walls are or how posh the environment happens to be. Ethics of the medical profession, competence, quality, and attitude of the staff are some of the factors that determine if a hospital is reliable or not. I will always recommend that you should find out how experienced the doctors and nurses employed in a hospital are, as well as how customer centric they are before choosing that hospital.

Health is wealth and you can only strive for success if you are alive and healthy. In Nigeria, so many people have been sent to early graves due to lack of experience and carelessness of doctors. Others have died because of obsolete machines that were no longer effective. I believe that it is only proper for everyone to be entitled to adequate and reliable health care. Nigerians deserve better.

LESSONS:

- Doctors and nurses should be more attentive to their patients
- Hospitals should provide balanced diet for their patients
- Hospital hygiene is very important
- Doctors are not always right
- Nigerian government should begin to care about effective medical care for its citizens
- Health care matters
- Health is wealth

CHAPTER 21

MY WEIGHT LOSS JOURNEY

> "IF WE CAN GET PEOPLE TO FOCUS ON FRUITS AND
> VEGETABLES AND MORE HEALTHY FOODS, WE'LL BE
> BETTER IN TERMS OF OUR HEALTHCARE SITUATION "
> – TOM VILSACK

I am so glad that all over the world people are becoming more conscious of their health and making deliberate effort to eat healthy and exercise regularly. While still in Lagos, on my way to work, I saw many people jogging on the streets. It made me happy knowing that health equates wealth. I remember how I usually work out in my room, just before showering and getting ready for work. Exercising daily has become a way of life for me and I feel very awkward on the days I skip exercising to get to work on time. If I can exercise daily, you too can. We only have one life to live and our health is very important. Truth be told, maintaining a healthy diet, and exercising regularly will increase your life span.

I used to be very health conscious. This was in the 90s. Although I already had a child, I weighed about 150 pounds. At 5ft 6 inches tall, I was very healthy. My diet consisted mostly of fruits and vegetables and I made sure that my shopping list had only cholesterol free foods, low fat milk, zero percent yogurts and low sugar drinks. I skinned my chicken before cooking it. I drank skimmed milk until I came down with food poison from an expired bottle of milk.

When I developed health issues and had to undergo a fibroid surgery, I became less conscious of my weight. Complicated by an additional diagnosis of thyroid deficiency, I was placed on a strong medication that proved to be unnecessary. When the thyroid deficiency diagnosis was revealed to be a farce, I got rid of my diet plan. I was too happy to have survived that I could not be bothered any more about piling up weight. I began to devour every carbohydrate, beef, and chicken sausage I could afford. I suddenly remembered how much I love eating full continental breakfast. Bread and full grain rice were re-introduced to my dining table. I stopped exercising. The weight kept piling up until November, 2012 when I realized that my weight had sky rocketed up to 212 pounds.

That was just before I travelled on a trip to the United States. Previously, I thought that it was easier to pile up weight in Africa than in the United States because of the heavy carbohydrates and starchy foods eaten in Africa. When my friends introduced me to the wide variety of food in the US, I realized that I was wrong. Food was available in larger sizes. There were different kinds of chicken, dipped in variety of sauces. Burgers, ice creams, chocolates, milkshakes, all came in a wide variety of sizes and flavors. Delicious fruity and juicy Ice creams were sold in large containers. I fell in love with American ice cream and looked forward to splurging on it just as much as I enjoyed eating ice cream in Dubai each time I visited.

My home girl and childhood friend Gozie that I usually stayed with in the United States had teenage children. One day, they urged me to climb on a scale. I did, and was embarrassed to hear their chanting of Oohs and Aahs. I was thoroughly embarrassed. There and then, I decided to do something drastic about my weight. I chose not to wait until after my vacation before kicking off my weight loss plan. The first thing I did was to stop partaking in their frequently available, delicious chicken. I began an exercise and diet program that worked so fast and so well that it even surprised my greatest critics. That is why I have decided to share it with you in this book.

Gozie and her husband Ony tried to stop me by reminding me that I was on vacation. They urged me to relax and enjoy myself. I told them that I did not want a situation where I may not be able to fit into the front door of my house when I returned to Nigeria because of excessive weight gain. They laughed at me. They thought that I was joking and could not carry through with my plan but they were surprised by my determination. They tempted me with a large bucket of Blue Bunny ice cream, filled with nuts. I stunned them by taking only two spoons before dumping the ice cream in their freezer. I knew that it would be consumed before daybreak. I was relying on their sons who were in the habit of raiding their fridge at night when everyone else was asleep and I was right. The ice-cream was gone before morning.

Knowing that I was weighing over two hundred pounds made me more determined to give up fatty foods. Beef, ice cream, chicken, yogurt, pastries were all excluded from my diet. I maintained a diet of salads and fruits until I returned to Nigeria. In America, it was so easy for me to buy vegetables that were clean and packed in transparent bags. All I needed to do was open the plastic bags, pour their contents in a bowl, add some non-fat cream, strawberries, and grapes, and eat. I spent days shopping with absolutely nothing else but water in my tummy and apples that I tucked in my bag until I felt hunger pangs. At night, I drank herbal tea after eating more fruits. My friends could not understand how salad and fruits kept me going, but I survived on them, felt lighter and was quite happy with the progress I was making.

As soon as I returned to Nigeria, I picked up my skipping rope and started skipping. At first, it was difficult because. I had not skipped in several years. I could only manage fifty jumps and eventually increased it to one hundred jumps per day. In a few weeks, I advanced to two hundred jumps a day. Next, I did some aerobics then lay on the floor for my yoga moves and stomach stretches. I added fifty sit-ups and fifty press ups. This was done every day. I started by doing press - ups with my knuckles and it almost killed me. My knuckles turned black and my shoulders felt like they were falling off their hinges. I was in constant pain.

By February, I went to the hospital. After x-rays, the doctor recommended surgery. He said that surgery was necessary to correct the severe pain in my shoulders. I believed the aches could have resulted from the press ups I was doing everyday but the doctor insisted that the surgery was necessary. I was convinced that it was because of the exercises knowing that I was really stretching my limits. Considering my experience so far in Nigerian hospitals, I decided that I was not going to agree to any surgery. If I had to go for a surgery, it will be outside Nigeria. I therefore chose to obtain a second opinion from another doctor.

I called a doctor friend of mine in the United Kingdom who demanded for a medical report from the orthopedic surgeon in Nigeria. You can imagine how shocked I was to realize that the Nigerian doctor mentioned nothing about the surgery he recommended for me in the medical report. I scanned and sent it by e mail to the doctor in the UK. I had gone ahead to discuss the need for a surgery with him and he was equally surprised by the discrepancy between what was in the report and what we earlier discussed. He said that surgery was not necessary. He said that if the pain continued, I should use a neck collar. He also advised me to exclude press ups from my exercise. My knuckles remained black for a while. They were very much like that of the Isaleko (Lagos Island) women who bleach their skin with harsh creams, ending up with "iru fanta, okpa coke" (yellow face and black legs). I gave up the press-ups but continued with other forms of exercise and a healthy diet. I applied aloe vera on my darkened knuckles to restore my skin color. By this time, I had already lost about eighteen pounds. I altered my wake-up time from 4.30 in the morning to 4am, gaining sufficient time for morning prayers and my 30 minutes daily work out. In a short while, the size of my stomach and rear side reduced. I had obviously shed some remarkable weight but it came with a price. My dresses became too big for me, my skirts and pants literally dropped off my waist. I sent a few of my favorite clothes to my tailor for re - shaping and gave out the rest to friends that were my previous size.

I had two tailors, Tony, and Emem. Tony was very good in fixing foreign clothes including jeans trousers and suits, while Emem had so much talent in making traditional African clothes for women. Tony was such an expert that he would finish altering the clothes without any indication of his having done so, except for failing to properly iron and fold the clothes before returning them to me. When all my effort to make him handle his customers' clothes in a professional manner failed, I resolved to always send my clothes to the laundry once he was done working on them. Tony was a petite man with an over bloated ego who was always boasting loudly about how he trained as a fashion designer in the United States. I never bothered asking him why he returned to Nigeria, knowing how rich he would have been if he had remained in the US. Each time I gave him clothes to fix, he always did an amazing job. I learned to patiently bear his over bloated ego trips and blabbing despite his excessive charges.

Emem was a very talented and humble young lady. She was so intelligent that all you needed to do was show her a picture of someone wearing the style you wanted to replicate and provide your fabric.

You Too Can Overcome Life's Challenges

Emem always succeeded in producing such an amazing replica of the original design that when placed beside it, you may never be able to differentiate between the two. Emem was so gifted that I declared her a champion when she made six elegant outfits for my elder sister who visited Nigeria from the United States. The clothes were ready within two weeks. My sister was so impressed that she sang her praises all the way back to the US.

The most interesting thing about Emem was that she worked alone. She used to sit in her dingy shop which was in a densely populated part of Lagos, making beautiful clothes for wealthy people. She was her own designer, tailor, accountant, customer service personnel, and marketer. Although largely uneducated, Emem had a fantastic public relations approach to business. When necessary, she often found time to go and collect clients' fabrics from their homes when necessary. She also went shopping for additional fabrics for her clients. All these she did without grumbling. Emem willingly went an extra mile to achieve customer satisfaction. I gave Emem some lace fabrics to make for me and completely forgot for about three months. I had just returned to Lagos from my sojourn in Ghana and bought some ceremonial Swiss laces that I needed for wedding ceremonies. I was a manager in an insurance company and was required to lead my marketing team to events. It was important for me to dress well.

They were very expensive lace fabrics. They were the latest in vogue at the time. There were three sets, with equally expensive blouses. I was new to my job and had a huge target to meet. I got so busy that I completely forgot about the clothes. Within those three months I lost contact with Emem. Although she was in constant touch with some of my friends, she made no effort to call or reach me. What happened next is a story that I love to recount and one that reminds me of how God can influence our everyday life with his enormous power. I remembered my fabrics in a very miraculous manner. It was on a Divine Mercy Sunday, a special day in the calendar of the Catholic Church. During Mass, when the priest raises the monstrance which houses the consecrated Eucharistic Host (where Jesus Christ dwells) It is believed that every request made by a believer is granted.

I had been a firm believer in this practice for years and always looked forward to being in church on Divine Mercy Sundays. It always gave me an opportunity to unburden my heart and make my request directly to God. When the priest raised the monstrance, accompanied by the sweet sound of the bell, I and the rest of the congregation fell on our knees. When I looked up and was about making my request, a vision of my lace fabrics appeared before me and I heard a voice saying, "Ifeoma, where are your clothes?" For a moment, I wondered, my clothes? Then it all came to me and I gasped, oh my God! The woman kneeling next to me turned and scowled at me like I was an impudent child breaking the rule of silence that no one dared to question at such times in the Catholic Church. It was a solemn, quiet time. If you dropped a pin on the floor of the church, the sound was sure to echo.

From church, I drove to my sister Chizo's house. When I told her about the vision I saw in church, she said I should quickly call Emem to know if my clothes were still safe. I called a very good friend of mine that is also Emem's client who confirmed that she had been in touch with Emem but knew nothing about my clothes. She informed me of a recent fire outbreak in Emem's house. She and my sister were almost certain that the flames consumed my clothes but something in me refused to believe it. My conviction was because I knew that if the fire in Emem's apartment destroyed my clothes; they would have appeared charred instead of as intact as they were in the vision that I saw in church. That was all the confirmation I needed to know that my clothes were safe. God does not tell lies, I concluded. Ignoring all skepticism, I picked up my cell phone, and called Emem.

She apologized profusely for not contacting me for three months and explained that the fire incident destroyed her home. She said that she was still recovering from her loss. She confirmed that my clothes were safe and promised to drop them off at my friend's house the following day. Although she requested an additional payment which she said was spent on buying accessories, I was only too happy to recover my clothes that I refused to make it an issue. Emem delivered my clothes. She surprised everyone that thought she had stolen and sold them to make money. She was able to prove beyond any iota of doubt that she was a woman of integrity.

Emem remained my dressmaker until the day I called her number and got the most unanticipated shock. The man that answered the call introduced himself as her brother and calmly informed me that Emem was dead. I screamed in utter disbelief. He said that she died two weeks before my call. When I heard the full story of how Emem was murdered, my heart filled with disgust. She was a victim of what I refer to as the "I want to marry" syndrome. She was a typical young lady struggling to succeed. Although without a formal education, she had a rare talent that God had bestowed on her and she did her very best to serve her community with it. I heard that a certain young man she was dating proposed marriage and she gladly accepted. He insisted on pre - marital sex, saying that he wanted her to conceive before they could fix a date for the wedding.

Emem, who had been abstaining from sex as a true Christian woman, allowed herself to be deceived and started sleeping with him. It was while trying to get pregnant, that she contacted HIV/AIDS. Emem developed complications and died. The inexplicable and very annoying aspect of this distressing story was that the man that destroyed her life survived. He is probably still prowling the streets of Lagos in search of his next victim. Everyone that knew how hard Emem worked and the much she would have been able to accomplish if she had not encountered this man, mourned her. She was a young, talented, and very hard-working girl. I missed her expertise so much that I searched for months before I found another tailor almost as skillful as Emem.

I continued my weight loss routine to the admiration of my friends and coworkers who could not stop discussing the progress I was making. I reduced my food consumption to one major daily meal. I gave up full grain rice and settled for Basmati rice, which I ate once or twice in a month. My diet consisted mainly of boiled and baked potatoes with tomato sauce made with non-cholesterol oil. I ate beans, eggs and drank water as if it was my favorite drink. Fizzy drinks and soda were totally out of my diet. By the end of March, 2013, I was down to 183 pounds. From size 18 plus and approaching size 20, I came down to British size 14. Although it took a lot of effort and I was over stressed, it really was worth it. Not only did I feel like a new person, some of my clients had to take a second look at me before they recognized me. I made herbal tea and unsweetened drinks my best friends. I discovered a brand of herbal tea that worked for me and stuck to it. In the past, I used to make herbal tea with a cup full of water, until I realized that it works better with less water.

As difficult as my weight watch program was, I persisted. Being long past my forties, losing my love handles (extra fat on the tummy) was a herculean task. I struggled each new day and it seemed almost impossible for me to maintain my newly achieved sexy figure. When Adaora came home and saw me for the first time since I started working out, she screamed in excitement "Mummy, you look sexy." This was at the airport where I had gone to pick her up. She twirled me around to admire my pretty figure, we laughed together in delight. I knew the joy she displayed was in appreciation of the effort I made. Being her hero, I will do it all over again to make her happy. Shedding weight has never been easy for me. If I could do it, you too can.

When you succeed in losing weight, you feel like a new person. You become more energetic and you can try out new clothes that you would have been embarrassed to wear in the past. You become more courageous and your self-esteem increases. I have decided to stay healthy by eating right and exercising regularly. If you enjoy looking good like I do, you need to start exercising. You should also change your diet. Eat more fruits and vegetables, while avoiding fatty foods.

LESSONS:

- If you want to live a long and fulfilled life, love yourself and take good care of your body
- Your health is your responsibility and to be successful, you need to be healthy
- You can only think of making money when you are healthy
- Losing weight requires a lot of determination
- You can always create time for exercise
- Adopt a healthy diet and exercise regularly
- There is always a price to pay for everything good
- Great talent always shines through

CHAPTER 22

BE PREPARED

> FIRST ASK YOURSELF: WHAT IS THE WORST THAT CAN
> HAPPEN? THEN PREPARE TO ACCEPT IT. THEN PROCEED
> TO IMPROVE ON THE WORST.
> – DALE CARNEGIE

One of the first lessons I learned as a teenager was to always be prepared for whatever comes my way. This is the Boys Scouts' solemn creed which I became acquainted with as a member of the Nigerian Girls' Guide Association. Apart from learning how to obey laws, I learned how to always be prepared for anything that may come up. As my life evolved, the training I received contributed to my ability to cope with the challenges I faced. I continued to learn new facts of life as I journeyed along. Just like I did not know that a hospital could be substandard, I also never expected a hotel, which is supposed to be a place of relaxation and comfort, to be less than perfect.

My experience in one of the so called five-star hotels in Lagos taught me how to anticipate the worst. Since then, instead of thinking that if I checked into a hotel in any third world country, I would receive value for my money, I always prepare for whatever comes up. Hotels in Nigeria and other developing countries operate as strict moneymaking ventures. A hotel is supposed to be a hospitality place where the welfare of the guests should be paramount in the minds of the owners, and their employees. When a lodger pays for an accommodation in a hotel, he exchanges money for comfort. When he fails to get the desired comfort, he feels cheated.

Have you ever checked into a hotel in Nigeria? If you have you not, better be prepared for an unpleasant adventure. Most of the hotels are substandard. They may at best be described as painted monuments. They are beautiful on the outside, but deplorable within. Although some of the hotels' managements make deliberate effort to ensure that they are up to international standards, there are still noticeable gaps. I was inspired by an experience I had in one of the biggest hotels in the city of Lagos to write a poem that I would like to share with you.

RELAXATION PLACES

HOTELS SPRING UP
OLD ONES RESURRECTED
REDESIGNED AND FRESHLY PAINTED
NEWLY DISCOVERED
MONEY MAKING MACHINES
EXTRA ROOMS
STRETCHED BEYOND CAPACITY

PLACES OF RELAXATION
ESCAPE FROM HUSTLE AND BUSTLE OF REALITY
SERENE ATMOSPHERE
APPRECIABLE AMBIENCE
COOLING RACKED NERVES
BRINGING US BACK TO NORM
BEFORE WE RETREAT
INTO OUR STRESS PACKED WORLD

BEAUTIFULLY DESIGNED AESTHETICS
OF THE EXTERIOR
OFTEN A SHAM
INADEQUATE PACKING SPACES
ILL-MANNERED RECEPTIONISTS
IMPATIENT JANITORS
WARM LOBBY
BUT THE GREATEST SHOCK LIES WITHIN

PREVIOUSLY WHITE SHEETS LEERING
EX WHITE TOWELS STARING
FROM THE BATHROOM
HUMIDITY ARRESTS YOU
AS YOU SEARCH HOPELESSLY
FOR A REMOTE CONTROL
RAMSHACKLE, RUSTY REFRIGERATOR
CAMPS IN A CORNER
A STENCH FILLS THE ROOM
AND YOU GRAB A PHONE
ROOM SERVICE TO THE RESCUE

POWER GOES OFF AND THE GENERATOR COMES ON
FRIDGE REPLACED; WHITE TOWEL FOUND
FIXED CHANNEL YOU REALLY DO NOT CARE TO WATCH
HUMS IN A FAMILIAR TONE
SHOWER TIME
PRECIOUS LIQUID RUNNING THROUGH YOUR TIRED LIMBS
OH NO! THIS CANNOT BE
TAPS GONE DRY
IFEOMA NDIOLO

The poem aptly sums up how unpleasant staying in these hotels can be. Although they are tagged five-star hotels, they do not deserve a three-star label. If you have visited developed countries and even a few African (third world countries) and stayed in their five-star hotels, which some of them humbly classify as three stars, you will certainly downgrade these hotels. Five-star hotels are supposed to be luxurious hotels of leisure where facilities do not just exist as part of the décor but function effectively. Travelers check into five-star hotels when they want to be able to relax and rejuvenate. That is the kind of satisfaction not guaranteed in most hotels in Nigeria. The power challenge makes it impossible for commercial enterprises to run as effectively as they should.

From the entrance, you would see a notice telling you that your cars are being parked at "owners," risk. This is a warning that the hotel's management will not be responsible should anything unpleasant happen to your vehicle, even within its premises. You walk into the lobby and the receptionist welcomes you with an obviously fake smile. If you are lucky, a bellboy helps you with your luggage, or you drag it along with you as you walk into the elevator. After checking in, you may be kept waiting for fifteen to twenty minutes for your room to be ready. That may leave you wondering why it was not cleaned after the previous occupant left. When you arrive at your floor, you may be lucky to find clear indicators to where your room is located. Sometimes, you find out that the signs are so confusing that you keep going back and forth until you finally locate your room. While some hotels use the American system of first floor, which is the ground floor, others prefer the British style of first floor being the level after the ground floor. Either way, it helps to confirm the exact position of your room before you go further.

The warm air hits you and you search for the switch to turn on the air conditioner. If you are lucky, the bellboy will locate and turn it on for you before collecting his tip. If after thirty minutes, your room remains warm, pick up the phone, and call the receptionist. Request for the maintenance to be informed. It is always better to ask for a change of room if the air conditioner is faulty. This is because you may have to wait for another twenty-four hours or more before someone turns up to fix it. Check the bathroom. If the toilet bowl was white and turned brownish or cream, it is most likely due to inadequate maintenance. Ensure that bath, hand, and floor towels have been provided.

Check the shower curtain and be sure it is long enough to prevent water spillage. Check for toilet paper. Most times, there are no extras. Check the water heater to ensure that it is working. Turn it on to ensure that there will be hot water for your bath. Check the shower to confirm that it is functioning. You may need to request a bucket and plastic bowl for scooping water. These are acceptable alternatives in Nigeria. Shampoo, hand cream, shower cap are bonuses and come in various containers and brand names. If you find some in your room, you dare not complain about their quality. The room may be stale or damp. Do not open the door or windows or you will be inviting mosquitoes to dinner. This means you are prepared for a bout of malaria.

Done with the bathroom, check the Television for your favorite channels, you will most likely discover that you have just a few options. Most times, you are restricted to one music channel, CNN, African Magic, and some local channels. If the pictures are not clear, make another call for them to be properly tuned. There is a possibility that the last occupier of your room did not care about watching TV. The phone book or telephone directory is normally in a conspicuous corner, beside the telephone box. If the numbers are confusing, call the receptionist to transfer your call to the appropriate extension.

Phew!

You have done a lot since you arrived, time to relax? I honestly do not think so.

Find out what time the kitchen closes for the day. Then, ask if there is a laundry service available for your use and request the price list. Please, do not assume that the fridge works even if you hear a humming sound. Check the fridge. Open it, and take note of its contents. Be mindful of the drinks, chocolates, and cookies that are in the fridge. Remember, you must account for anything you take. Nothing in the fridge is free. Be prepared to pay for everything you take unless you checked into a high-profile room or luxury penthouse. There, you may receive a complimentary bottle of wine. Executive suites in Nigeria are always fully booked and paid for, even when they are unoccupied. Politicians, oil magnates, and money bags reserve them for themselves and their special guests. They pay the bills regularly with their ill–gotten wealth. Their bills run into millions of Naira. In hotel business, money truly speaks. If you want a special room reserved, you must book ahead and pay or you will find out that there will be no available room when you arrive. Do not bother finding out who reserved the special rooms, who pays for them or what they are used for. Fake names and aliases are often used and no one scrutinizes if it is their mistresses,' relations or business partners that occupy the rooms.

The menu or food list lies close to the telephone. You may see a very long list split into starters, main courses, and deserts. You may also find drinks of various descriptions. Do not assume that all the food and drinks listed are available. When you call the restaurant to place an order, the response may be "we don't have it." You could mention three different items before you receive a yes and usually there are no explanations or apologies. It is best not to expect any. Find out how long it will take to prepare your preferred dish before ordering. The restaurant staff may inform you that the food will be ready in about thirty to forty-five minutes, which sometimes runs into an hour. While waiting, try to relax, take a nap, or watch something on the television. When the food is ready, the room service staff will knock on your door. Remember to check the tray to ensure that everything you requested, including water comes with your order. Do not rely on the fridge because there may not be any bottle of water in it. Also, ensure that cutlery, serviette, and tooth picks are included. Go through the bill and confirm that it is accurate before signing it. Enjoy your meal! If it is disgusting, keep it to yourself and plan to dine elsewhere. In smaller hotels, you can buy your meals from somewhere else but the so-called three- or five-star hotels do not allow it. The only option open to you is to find a nice restaurant nearby where you can go for your meals. When you are done, if you want the tray removed, call room service. Alternatively, take it outside your door by yourself or it will remain in your room until the following day. You do not want to wake up with the stench of stale food.

In smaller hotels, the taps hardly run due to power supply issues or break down of water pumping machines. It is either their generators are too small to pump water to the rooms or the bigger generators have developed technical fault and are undergoing repairs. Remember, you are in Nigeria where generators are the main source of power supply for every household and business, while the government supplies only ten to twenty percent of electricity consumption. If there is no water, call the reception or housekeeping to request for water and please specify if you want it cold, warm, or hot. An employee of the hotel will deliver it to you in a bucket. If the taps are running and the water is clean, it is your lucky day. However, do not assume that the tap will continue to run until you finish bathing. It just may run dry on you.

One day, when I was staying in one of the best hotels in Victoria Island, Lagos, I was in the bath when the taps suddenly stopped running. This was in the middle of my shower. I had just finished lathering my body and had to sit on the tub, cursing and moaning to myself for as long as it took before the water started flowing again. It was a very unpleasant experience. Despite taking every possible precaution to avoid a repeat of such an experience, it happened to me again. I had to towel dry the soap on my body, climbed out of the bath, sat, and waited for thirty long minutes before a hotel staff was able to organize water for me to finish bathing. He apologized profusely but it did not make me feel any better. I learned my lesson. When there is power outage, a lot can go wrong even in five-star hotels. The best option is to sit still and stay calm for as long as possible until the power generator comes on. Since then, I always include a torch light in my bag whenever I check into a hotel in Nigeria. You never know what will happen next and it is always better to be prepared.

Something else you need to watch out for in hotels are the bed sheets. If they are supposed to be white and they are not, please request a change of sheets. They just may be reserving the real white ones for the guests that complain. Also, check the pillows to ensure that they are suitable for sensitive necks, especially if you are not used to sleeping with hard pillows. You may find out that some of the pillows are as hard as a rock and will give you a stiff neck by the following morning. Do not leave any luxurious item; jewelry or money in your room and assume that it is secure. Always use the safe deposit box provided either in your room or at the reception, which can be locked up. Failing to do so means that should a robbery occur; you cannot hold anyone responsible for your loss. It is always wiser to confirm that the hotel you choose has an active insurance policy that covers burglary and theft before checking in. In the absence of an insurance policy, you are limited to accepting whatever compensation the hotel management decides to offer in the event of a loss, which will totally be at their discretion.

If hotel owners and managements make deliberate effort to improve on the quality of service their establishments deliver, it will positively affect their rating and increase their revenue. Beyond that, their clients will be delighted and more tourists will be attracted to Nigeria. Knowing that there will be world – class hotels where guests can feel at home always encourages tourism. Hotels are places of relaxation, away from home, where travelers are willing to pay adequately for services rendered. Please note the key phrase - services rendered. Expectations are usually high. The last thing any hotel guest is willing to tolerate is any form of inconvenience. Hotel workers should therefore make every possible effort to ensure that their guests are happy; bearing in mind how adequately they pay for the services they receive. Training and retraining of hospitality staff always help in resetting their mindset. It is important for the staff to understand that the safety, comfort, and well-being of the guests are what really matters. A hotel's outward appearance or how recently the walls were painted is always a secondary consideration.

As the world increasingly evolves into a global village, hotel owners in Nigeria should keep up with developments in the hospitality industry worldwide. In addition to re -branding and collaborating with notable hotels in developed countries, they should emulate their service delivery expertise.

There have been instances where robbery occurred in Nigerian hotels and the guests woke up the following morning wondering who provided information to the thieves on which rooms to raid. Hotel owners should investigate the quality of the individuals they employ. While a lodger is staying in a hotel, their lives are truly in the hands of the staff.

The Hospitality business remains a very lucrative business. There is no reason why unqualified individuals, who are probably money launderers and drug peddlers, should continue to see hotel ownership as a means of concealing their illegal activities. Some of them continue to set up monstrous structures in the name of hotels which eventually rot away, while they focus on their nefarious activities. To them, owning a hotel is just a way of utilizing the massive funds in their possession. They pose as business entrepreneurs to avoid the criminal investigation agencies. Such hotels are so easy to detect and can be seen littering the streets of major cities in Nigeria.

In a country like Nigeria where opportunities for legitimate business abound, such hotel owners should find other ways of utilizing their buildings. If other entrepreneurs and some hotel owners have succeeded in doing genuine business, nothing stops them from doing the same. They should find out what they are passionate about and start on a smaller scale. The business will eventually grow and they will experience fulfillment.

> "A SUCCESSFUL LIFE IS ONE THAT IS LIVED THROUGH
> UNDERSTANDING AND PURSUING ONE'S OWN PATH, NOT
> CHASING AFTER THE DREAMS OF OTHERS."
>   – CHIN- NING GHU

LESSONS:

- Be always prepared
- Cars parked in hotel premises should be under the care of the hotel management
- Training of hospitality staff is very important
- While in a hotel, use a safe deposit box
- Safety, comfort, and well-being of hotel guests are what really matters
- Customer satisfaction is what makes a hotel successful

CHAPTER 23

DISCOVER AND DEVELOP YOUR TALENT

> "I AM AN ORDINARY MAN WHO WORKED HARD TO DEVELOP
> THE TALENT I WAS GIVEN. I BELIEVED IN MYSELF, AND I
> BELIEVE IN THE GOODNESS OF OTHERS."
> - MUHAMMAD ALI

God gave talent to each one of us. Your talent distinguishes you from the next person. Your talent may be totally different from mine, just as other people's talents differ from yours. It is however the duty of each person to discover and develop his talent. If you start developing your talent once you become aware of it, you will be better positioned to become a successful person. Your talent is where your passion truly lies. You will find out that it comes naturally to you and it is something you enjoy doing. You may never know how successful you can be until you develop your talent. If your talent is not nurtured, groomed, and developed, it may wither and die. When you have discovered your talent, try your possible best to obtain the required training needed to effectively utilize it.

If you like cooking, you probably should enroll into a catering school where you can train to be a chef. After training, you can then pick up a job in a restaurant. One day, you may end up becoming the owner of a world class restaurant. If you like meeting new people, making friends and know that you can easily influence people, then you should go for marketing or sales. If f you like fashion, dressing up yourself and others, then you can start learning how to design and make clothes. While designing can come naturally to you, you still need to understand the fabrics and materials required for the clothes you will design. Training for a profession prepares you for the competition ahead. Apart from sharpening your knowledge, it humbles you. You will always remember that other people were there before you and no matter how good you thought you were; you had to learn from someone else. It also exposes you to multiple ways of growing your business.

In corporate organizations, most often than not, men and women that excel are those that are employed in their areas of competence which often align with their talents. These are the round pegs in round holes. It is not the same as when someone picks up a job in a field that he is totally unsuitable for. He becomes a round hole in a square peg and would most likely find himself struggling with his duties. He will be surprised to find his colleagues who are properly positioned being more excited about their jobs and performing much better.

If you want to enjoy your job, make sure it is in line with your passion and talent, otherwise it will be boring to you. Whether you are prepared or not, your talent will propel you into utilizing it, long before it yields an income for you.

I have always enjoyed reading and writing. Initially, I thought that I started writing after graduating from the university until my sister Chizo reminded me that while I was in secondary school, I was already writing. I remember that I toyed with the idea of writing songs and even recorded some songs, but forgot that I wrote poems and short stories. Recently, I was on a lunch date with a school mate of mine who recalled some of the poems I wrote while we were on campus. I wonder what happened to those poems. Then, I was totally ignorant of how to develop my talents and was more focused on acquiring a university degree. I must have lost so many creative ideas that were never recovered and I bet this has happened to so many others like me.

It is always better to start developing your talent as soon as you recognize it. Once I became aware of my passion for writing, I began to develop it. I received lots of encouragement from May Ellen Ezekiel (MEE), the late publisher of the highly respected Classique magazine. Unknowingly, she gave my creative life the push it required when she accepted and published my poems in her magazine. That was when I started collating my manuscripts and looking for a publisher. It took years before I could find anyone that was willing to even look at my work. I had to wait for a decade before I succeeded in publishing my first book. The delay in finding a publisher and the frustrating waiting period never discouraged me.

DISCOVER AND DEVELOP YOUR TALENT

Since my first book was published, I have never stopped writing. I have found out that I really cannot stop. What propels me to write is beyond me and is much greater than what I can control. That perhaps explain why despite the unfavorable social and economic environment in which I was struggling to survive, I managed to squeeze out time to write. Although I was living in a society where progress was obstructed by constant power outage, I continued to write. Sacrificing my social life, I continued to write. There were times that I finished writing a poem in the dark with a torchlight while waiting for the generator to start. I have been approached by some people who were curious to know how I managed to write and why I kept writing even when it was obvious that the income from my books were not encouraging.

It is often difficult for people to understand that having received such an unusual gift from God, I had no choice but to allow myself to be used as a vessel for achieving God's purpose. Writing makes me happy. You can never begin to imagine the joy I receive from knowing how people enjoy reading my poems and stories. The thrill they get is more satisfying than any amount of money anyone can offer me. That does not stop me from feeling frustrated with the lack of interest in reading and economic hardship which makes it very difficult to sell books. Despite the challenges, there are always people who appreciate creativity and who are always willing to support writers. I have been lucky to have met some of them and quite grateful that they encouraged me.

Developing and utilizing your talent has a lot of advantages. It can pay your bills and elevate you to a higher level. A talented person will always be recognized and appreciated beyond his immediate community. Through your talent you can even become an ambassador for your country. This has become the privilege of so many Nigerian actors, musicians, and footballers. Some came from very poor homes but were fortunate to have been given opportunities for their talents to be recognized. Actors like Olu Jacobs, Joke Silva, Taiwo Lycett, Genevieve Nnaji, Omotola Jalade Ekeinde and many others have without doubt enjoyed the fruits of their talents. In Nigerian football, reference is often made to Kanu Nwankwo, Mikel Obi, and Peter Odemwingie. These are highly talented Nigerians who have stood out on the international arena. In music, there are Nigerian musicians like P Square, Davido, and Flavor. Writers like Chinua Achebe, Cyprain

You Too Can Overcome Life's Challenges

Ekwensi, Wole Soyinka, Chimamanda Adichie and many other Nigerians have become worldwide acknowledged literary giants. It is not an impossible feat to achieve. You too can develop your talent and enjoy the benefit that comes from doing what you know how to do best.

> "YOUR TALENT IS GOD'S GIFT TO YOU. WHAT YOU DO WITH IT IS YOUR GIFT BACK TO GOD."
> – LEO BASCALGIA

LESSONS:

- Talent differs from one individual to another
- Your talent is where your passion truly lies
- You are only a tool being used by God for your talent to shine through
- Your talent will propel you into utilizing it
- Training makes you better
- Training humbles you
- Apart from financial independence, there is a lot more you can benefit from developing your talent
- Do not be discouraged by challenges
- Your talent will always shine through

CHAPTER 24

ATTITUDE IS EVERYTHING

> "IT'S NOT WHAT HAPPENS TO YOU THAT DETERMINES HOW FAR YOU WILL GO IN LIFE; IT IS HOW YOU HANDLE WHAT HAPPENS TO YOU."
> – ZIG ZIGLAR

It has often been said that the basic difference between people who succeed and those that do not is their attitude to the events that occur in their lives and around them. A person's attitude simply means his disposition. It is largely determined by his state of mind and how he perceives situations. His perception is often responsible for his opinion and how he reacts to situations.

We all face challenges. Our understanding of what we encounter determines how we react to them. For as long as we live in a world where we must share space with other people, events will continue to happen around us that we cannot totally control. Our ability or otherwise to shield ourselves from being influenced by the events taking place around us is what determines how they influence our life and the lives of our dependents. If you allow situations around you to dictate your decisions and behavioral patterns, you will succumb to character sway, frustration, and misery. If you can remain consistent, refusing to be manipulated and controlled by environmental factors, then you are on your way to being successful. Success does not come from dancing to the tune of time and season. Rather, success comes from staying focused, refusing to allow circumstances to distract you, and keeping your eyes on the finishing line; while consistently leaping over the hurdles on your path to achieve pre - determined goals.

Employees, who arrive at their offices with positive mental attitude, often succeed better than those who only see their job as a tool for their selfish needs. The positive thinking ones recognize that they are there to make a living and are therefore determined to add value to their establishments. For some others, once there is a challenge and their expectations are no longer being met by their employers, they spend most of their time converging in clusters, moaning, and groaning about the situation instead of getting the job done. These are workers that easily get frustrated. Their favorite phrases are it is not possible, it cannot be done, I cannot do it. They are negative thinking people who see a mountain in every molehill. They complain and lament all day. They are so involved in negativity that they fail to appreciate any effort made by their employers to improve their working conditions. They have a mindset, believe what they think and it shows in the way they approach their duties. They surrender to failure before making sufficient effort which is why they rarely succeed.

These are the people you and I see walking around every day with sagging shoulders and deep frown on their faces. They hardly smile because nothing ever makes them happy.

Men and women with this kind of mentality are not good for business and are worse for relationships. In business, they would rather maintain the existing status quo instead of thinking outside the box. They are not creative and are often unable to add value. They are more interested in resisting any effort towards changing the existing modalities than introducing innovative methods of achieving goals. They are so used to the old order and would rather have things remain exactly as they are. Their situation is usually pathetic. Change unsettles them and they cannot really cope with it. Their ideas are archaic and mundane. They have a mindset and no matter how much you try to convince them that there could be a bright light at the end of the dark tunnel, you will be wasting your time. They would rather see you as the dreamer who thinks he can change the world and condemn you instead of allowing you to air your views. It is either they avoid you or they do their possible best to castigate you. Organizations with less workers like this succeed better than others.

A positive attitude is everything. It is like a ray of sunshine within a heavy rainfall. It makes you see possibilities where there seems to be none. It makes you get up and go even when you would rather be on your bed. It makes you dare and when you fail, it makes you go back and try again. People with positive attitude always see a bright light in the horizon and keep reaching out for it. When they are falling, they hold on to the branch of the nearest available tree and somehow manage to spring back up. They are often able to swim to the shores when others would have drowned. They fight to win and even when they fail, get back on their feet, again, in the shortest possible time. They keep striving to succeed. They are leaders and not followers. They command respect and exude authority. They are fearless and are willing to take risks. These are the kind of people truly needed by every organization to stay ahead of their competitors.

We all need to work on our attitude. While facing recurring daily woes, political and economic challenges which require determined and structured efforts to break down financial and societal barriers, a positive attitude is what we really need to excel.

When I developed a strong faith in God, my attitude to life changed. I began to see things differently. A glass that I would have previously seen as half empty became half full. Nothing was considered unachievable for me. This change in attitude helped me a great deal as I struggled with training Adaora in school and paying huge fees for her as a foreign student in Ghana. I was never afraid. Even when I had no idea where her school fees would come from, I remained hopeful. I remember how she used to look at me and wonder what my plans were. She knew exactly how much I had in each of my bank accounts and wondered why I never worried about money. As we skipped through the hurdles in our lives, she also developed a positive attitude.

> "CULTIVATE AN OPTIMISTIC MIND, USE YOUR IMAGINATION, ALWAYS CONSIDER ALTERNATIVES, AND DARE TO BELIEVE THAT YOU CAN MAKE POSSIBLE WHAT OTHERS THINK IS IMPOSSIBLE."
> – RODOLFO COSTA

LESSONS:

- Your disposition determines your reaction
- Character sway, frustration and misery arise out of our inability to control our reaction to situations

You Too Can Overcome Life's Challenges

- Success does not come from dancing to the tune of time and season
- Success comes from staying focused, refusing to allow circumstances to distract you, and keeping your eyes on your goal
- When you easily surrender to failure, you rarely succeed.
- People with negative mental attitude are not good for business and are even worse for relationships
- A positive mental attitude is like a ray of sunshine during a heavy rainfall
- A positive mental attitude makes you see possibilities where there seems to be none

It is my sincere hope that reading these true-life stories will further convince you that God truly lives and still performs miracles. Since I was able to rise above the challenges in my life and succeed in achieving my set goals, including single handedly training Adaora through medical school without any government loan or assistance, I strongly believe that You Too Can. Recently, Adaora asked me how I was able to find the money to pay her school fees. She said that she calculated her tuition and it came up to $65,000, not including other expenses like flight tickets, accommodation, groceries. She said that she could not come up with an answer. I reminded her that it was not because I had the means but only because I believed that it was possible, remained focused and trusted God. You have the power to propel yourself from your present state of life to a more fulfilling and more satisfying one. Dare to achieve and you will.

ABOUT THE AUTHOR

Ifeoma Ndiolo is an African writer from Enugu state in Nigeria. She has a bachelor's degree with combined honors in English and History from the University of Nigeria, Nsukka and an MBA from Delta State University.

She started her working life as a news reporter in a national TV station in Lagos, Nigeria and later worked as programs manager in a private TV station also in Lagos. She worked as a marketer in a bank for four years. She was also an insurance marketing manager for over fifteen years for three major insurance companies in Nigeria. She has managed the corporate and public relations of several organizations. She is a public relations and marketing consultant, as well as a life coach.

Ifeoma is a prolific writer who has written poetry, works of fiction, and non-fiction. Her previously published books are *Panorama* (a collection of poems), *Juggle the Dice* (short stories) and *Hidden Treasures of the Heart*. She also has two other collections of poems among her body of work, *Echoes from Within* and *Rhythms from the Heart* which were released via a self-publishing online platform.

Ifeoma produced and directed *Pawns*, a 26-episode television drama series which she created from one of the stories in her book, *Juggle the Dice*. *Pawns* was broadcast on several TV stations in Nigeria and many African countries through a contract with DSTV (Multichoice, South Africa). Ifeoma has been a youth and women's leader and a mentor to many now successful protégés. She is the proud mother of Dr. Adaora Brenda Irene Obi who is a consultant Psychiatrist in Scotland, United Kingdom.

Ifeoma currently lives in the United States and works in the healthcare industry. She is a registered insurance agent in North Carolina.

INDEX

You Too Can Overcome Life's Challenges

www.ingramcontent.com/pod-product-compliance
Lightning Source LLC
Chambersburg PA
CBHW022058020426
42335CB00012B/734